Contents

WITHDRAWN

Assessing the use and impact of Anti-Social Behaviour Orders

Briggs

and Ken Pease

First published in Great Britain in 2007 by The Policy Press

The Policy Press
University of Bristol
Fourth Floor, Beacon House
Queen's Road
Bristol BS8 1QU
UK

Tel no +44 (0)117 331 4054
Fax no +44 (0)117 331 4093
E-mail tpp-info@bristol.ac.uk
www.policypress.org.uk

© Roger Matthews, Helen Easton, Daniel Briggs and Ken Pease 2007

ISBN 978 1 84742 057 2

British Library Cataloguing in Publication Data
A catalogue record for this report is available from the British Library.

Library of Congress Cataloging-in-Publication Data
A catalog record for this report has been requested.

Cover image courtesy of iStockphoto®
Cover design by Qube Design Associates, Bristol
Printed in Great Britain by Latimer Trend, Plymouth

List of figures and tables

Figures

Tables

Preface

This report is based on a research study that was commissioned by the Anti-Social Behaviour Unit in the Home Office to assess the impact and effectiveness of Anti-Social Behaviour Orders (ASBOs). This work represents one of the few studies to date to be carried out on ASBOs, and aims to chart the development and use of ASBOs following recent legislative changes. Against a background of growing public concern about anti-social behaviour (ASB), the use of ASBOs has become widely identified as potentially the most significant sanction to address ASB. Its use, however, has been surrounded by considerable controversy, although the evidence on which this controversy is based is conspicuously limited. This research therefore aims to throw some light on these issues and to examine the attitudes and experiences of key agencies, witnesses, residents and, importantly, offenders. The research was conducted mainly in the South East of England, although parts of the Midlands were also included. It therefore provides a selective rather than a randomised or representative sample. However, the information gathered in the course of this research provides a useful and timely indication of the role, impact and effectiveness of ASBOs from the perspectives of the main parties most directly involved in their use.

Acknowledgements

A number of people have contributed to this research both directly and indirectly. We are grateful to all those agency representatives who have cooperated with this research by providing information and contacts, as well as taking the time to participate in interviews.

We would like to thank the community groups, witnesses and complainants who agreed to be interviewed or participate in focus groups. The 66 offenders who have been served with anti-social behaviour orders made up the largest constituent group and their involvement and cooperation was critical to the success of the project.

Introduction

Background

The initial deployment of Anti-Social Behaviour Orders (ASBOs) following the passing of the 1998 Crime and Disorder Act was much slower than anticipated. This was mainly attributed to a lack of familiarity with their use, the time and costs involved in processing cases and the uncertainty about their effects (Burney, 2002). Over the past few years, the number of ASBOs issued has grown rapidly (see Figure 1.1) and although there are considerable regional variations, the number of ASBOs reported to the Home Office by all courts in England and Wales up to the end of June 2005 was 6,497.

The 2002 Police Reform Act extended the right to apply for ASBOs to the British Transport Police and Registered Social Landlords. The Act also introduced Anti-Social Behaviour Orders on Conviction (CRASBOs), which may be imposed by the courts in addition to a sentence for a criminal offence involving anti-social behaviour, as well as interim ASBOs, which may be imposed relatively quickly before awaiting a full hearing (Home Office, 2003).

The availability of these measures has no doubt been influential in encouraging the greater use of ASBOs. The rapid increase in the number of ASBOs and CRASBOs issued suggests that a review of their effectiveness and impact is timely.

Figure 1.1: Number of ASBOs reported to the Home Office, 2000-05

Number of anti-social behaviour orders issued, as reported to the Home Office by all courts, by quarter, from 1st April 1999 to 30th June 2005

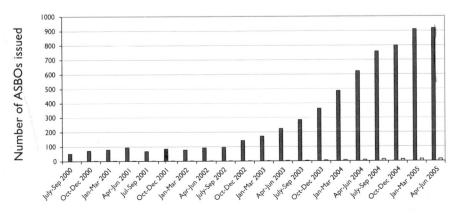

There has been much discussion in academic and public circles about the use of ASBOs recently, but there is limited empirical research (Squires and Stephen, 2005). This research was designed to provide an exploratory study of ASBOs and to examine the views and experiences of the three key parties involved – the agencies, the offenders and the victims.

The research aims to examine the implementation of ASBOs and their impact on the different types of offenders. It examines the role of the agencies involved in processing and issuing ASBOs; the impact on those given ASBOs, particularly in relation to their propensity to engage in anti-social and criminal behaviour; and the experience and concerns of victims and affected communities.

Recent research and publications on ASBOs

The first major piece of research on ASBOs was carried out by Siobhan Campbell (2002a). This research was based on the examination of 94 case files, 76 interviews with practitioners and 33 interviews with victims. The research focused on the role of the agencies and partnerships in processing ASBOs and in developing clearer procedures for handling cases. It was pointed out that the processing of ASBOs involved unnecessary bureaucracy, long delays and excessive costs. Although it is possible that Campbell's suggestions have helped to improve procedures, the growth of ASBOs on conviction has proved an alternative way of sidestepping the usual procedures adopted by Crime and Disorder Reduction Partnerships (CDRPs) around the country. Campbell drew attention to the fact that three quarters of those given ASBOs were under 21 years of age, that approximately one third of ASBOs were breached within a relatively short period of time and that almost half of those sentenced in court for breaching their order were given a custodial sentence. At the same time, the report notes that there were relatively low levels of monitoring and evaluation of ASBOs by CDRPs. Campbell also found that ASBOs worked more effectively when used in conjunction with a package of support. She drew attention to ways in which systematic breaches of orders could undermine the benefits gained during the application process, and found examples of where ASBOs had, in the short run at least, served to curb unruly behaviour. Her focus, however, was primarily on the role of agencies and the impact on communities rather than on the experiences of offenders.

In a supplementary publication directed mainly at practitioners, Campbell (2002b) suggests that if ASBOs are to be successful, they need to be targeted at the appropriate people. She also emphasised that the wording of the order needs to be carefully considered, the conditions specified in the order need to be rigorously formulated, the displacement of anti-social behaviour should be avoided wherever possible, and the monitoring of orders should be systematic. These general suggestions were also included in the London Anti-Social Behaviour Strategy (GLA, 2005), which noted that issuing an ASBO might further marginalise certain offenders and exacerbate their problems. Other research has pointed to the marginalised status of many of those given ASBOs. Elisabeth Burney (2002), for example, reported that 60 per cent of those issued ASBOs were people with mental and social problems, a factor that may also be related to the actual or perceived effectiveness of ASBOs and the appropriateness of their use.

The Home Affairs Committee (2005), which took evidence on the use of ASBOs, found that the concerns of those it interviewed regarding the use of ASBOs included suggestions that some orders carried inappropriate conditions and that they failed to address the support needs of offenders. The committee also expressed some concerns about the 'naming and shaming' of offenders, and the possibility that ASBOs provide a 'back-door' route into custody. While the Home Affairs Committee was generally supportive of the use of ASBOs, it called for more research to help clarify some of these issues and to provide a better evidence base on which to build future policy and practices.

Others factor that may influence the actual or perceived effectiveness of an ASBO are the conditions written into an order and the way that an order is enforced. Lord Justice Thomas (2005) suggests that some ASBO conditions have been deemed inappropriate, have been too widely drawn or have proven unenforceable. In a similar way, Floud (2005) identifies differences in the way ASBOs are monitored by housing departments and the police, which may also have an impact on the use and effectiveness of ASBOs.

Anti-Social Behaviour Orders have also been introduced in Scotland and a recent evaluation has indicated that, as in England and Wales, the number of ASBOs issued has increased significantly in recent years, rising from 57 in 2001/02 to 148 in 2003/04 (Scottish Executive, 2005). There are, however, two significant differences in the use of ASBOs in Scotland compared with England and Wales. The first was that in Scotland ASBOs are applied mainly to those living in social housing. The second is that nearly two thirds of ASBOs are issued to people over the age of 25. The level of breaches has been found to be relatively high, with as many as two thirds being breached within a year. However, unlike England and Wales, those breaching the conditions of an ASBO cannot be jailed. As in England and Wales, the duration of ASBOs varies considerably. However, 44 per cent are for an indefinite period.

A report published by the Runnymede Trust, entitled *Equal Respect* (Isal, 2006), bemoans the unavailability of ethnic data in relation to the use of ASBOs. The report is concerned with the potential disproportionate use of ASBOs against ethnic minorities and the extent to which ASBOs might be considered to be an appropriate sanction to deal with racial harassment. The report calls for a more detailed breakdown of the ethnicity of ASBO recipients in order that their use can be effectively monitored and made more transparent.

The report also points out that the failure to gather data on ethnicity is in contravention of section 95 of the 1991 Criminal Justice Act, which requires the government to assess the impact of its policies and practices on different ethnic groups. Although the author of the report notes that an ASBO is technically a civil procedure, the same principles should apply. The report suggests that there should be a thoroughgoing review of the ways in which ASBOs are used. Such a review, it is suggested, should include breaches as well as examining the types of support mechanisms that are used in conjunction with ASBOs. At the same time, the procedures for ethnic monitoring should be established and refined in order to determine how different ethnic groups experience and perceive the use of ASBOs.

One of the few studies that includes some information on the ethnicity of ASBO recipients is the research carried out in the King's Cross area of North London for the London Borough of Camden (Young et al, 2006). This study found that 37% of the ASBOs issued in the borough were given to African Caribbean males, although African Caribbeans make up approximately 8% of the population in Camden as a whole. Fifty-three per cent of those who received ASBOs were described as 'white', 6% were 'mixed race' and 4% were 'Asian'. It was not clear from this study, however, whether the disproportionate use of ASBOs for African Caribbean males was a function of discriminatory practices or differential involvement in offending.

The London Borough of Camden has issued by far the highest number of ASBOs in the London area. By the end of 2006, it had issued 218 ASBOs as part of an attempt to 'crack down' on anti-social behaviour (ASB), particularly in 'hotspots' such as King's Cross. The main target for the use of ASBOs was found to be street prostitution, drug use and drug dealing as well as begging. The justification given for the use of ASBOs against these and other groups was that experienced criminals were exploiting the loopholes in the criminal justice system, while sanctions like fines, rehabilitation orders and drug treatment orders were seen to have little effect. ASBOs were seen as a potentially effective way to sanction these criminals. The emphasis within the council, the report suggests, was on protecting the community rather than catering for the needs of offenders.

It became apparent in the course of the research, however, that there was a split between those agencies in the CDRP that generally supported the use of ASBOs and the more welfare-orientated agencies that felt that their use could be 'catastrophic', particularly when used in relation to street prostitutes, the homeless and substance misusers. Those who criticised the use of ASBOs argued that rather than resolving the problem they tended to displace vulnerable people, undermine established networks of support and make it difficult for people to access services within the borough. Concerns were also expressed by respondents in relation to the erosion of civil liberties and the right to freedom of movement. There were also concerns about the displacement of crime and anti-social behaviour both within the borough and to surrounding boroughs.

Breaches of orders was identified as a major issue with three out of four of the 25 individuals given ASBOs in the King's Cross area breaching the conditions of their order. Interestingly, it was noted that a significant number of these breaches occurred shortly after the order was granted and was seen in some cases as the ASBO recipients 'testing out' the 'validity' of the sanction. Breaches, it was reported, often resulted from entering the zone of exclusion or breaking the 'good behaviour' clause.

Although the report notes that there has been a considerable decline in the levels of ASBOs in the King's Cross area, particularly in relation to street prostitution and drug dealing, it is difficult to assess the impact of ASBOs because there has been a wide-ranging multimillion pound series of interventions focused on this area in the past few years. Therefore, although it is probably the case that the use of ASBOs has contributed to this outcome, their precise contribution remains unclear.

Another study that focuses on one specific location has been carried out by Laurence Koffman on East Brighton in Sussex (Koffman, 2006). His research found that Brighton and Hove accounted for almost half of the ASBOs issued in the whole of Sussex. Examining the case files of 28 individuals, the research investigated the background and situation of perpetrators as well as affording the opportunity to examine modes of interagency working. Koffman found that some 80% of ASBOs were given to people in this location who were 20 years of age or younger. ASBOs were seen by practitioners as a 'last resort', to be used for more persistent offenders.

The focus of the research was an assessment of whether the use of ASBOs could be considered 'appropriate', 'inappropriate' or 'equivocal'. Koffman estimates that approximately half of the ASBOs issued could be described as 'appropriate' in as much as the offender had engaged in serious and persistent offending and that there were no other available sanctions that were adequate or had not been used before. A quarter of ASBOs were described as 'equivocal' in as much as they were seen to provide some respite for the community, but there were doubts about whether an ASBO was the most cost-effective available sanction. In the remaining cases, it was felt that the use of an ASBO was inappropriate or that there was not enough information to judge.

Koffman points out that ASBOs were not used in East Brighton for dealing primarily with cases of nuisance, but that the majority were used for cases involving relatively serious forms of misconduct and offending. Many of the offenders given ASBOs, he notes, already had criminal records and in some cases were simultaneously being dealt with by the criminal justice system for other forms of misconduct. He points out that in some cases those given ASBOs suffered from severe personal, emotional and mental health problems such as Attention Deficit Hyperactivity Disorder, while he also notes that in a number of cases the parents of those issued with ASBOs also suffered from problems of physical or mental health. At the same time, he reports that almost half of the ASBO applications were not contested and that many cases were not defended as forcibly as they might have been.

The report by the National Audit Office on tackling anti-social behaviour (NAO, 2006) picks up on the theme of the inadequacy of available information on ASB measures, including ASBOs and the lack of formal evaluation. The report states:

> The absence of formal evaluation by the Home Office of the success of different interventions and the impact of providing support services in conjunction with interventions prevents local areas targeting interventions in the most efficient way to achieve the best outcome for the least cost. (NAO, 2006, p 5)

Thus, although there has been a considerable amount of money and resources directed to tackling ASB, there is little understanding of 'what works' out of the growing array of interventions introduced in recent years.

The National Audit Office report was based on 893 case files in six local areas, structured interviews with ASB coordinators in 12 local areas, focus groups in six local areas and 20 interviews with individuals who have received ASB interventions. Based on this data, the report claimed that ASB interventions were effective with the majority of offenders and that those who received ASBOs took longer than the other available sanctions to re-engage in ASB, although they could not control for the seriousness of offending of different individuals.

The report indicated that just under half of those receiving an ASBO had breached it, with a third of this group doing so five or more times. It reports that these breaches were not always dealt with in a timely manner and that in some cases victims were unwilling to come forward.

The research, however, only considered formal breaches and because of the relatively low number of ASBO recipients interviewed there was no account taken of the number of unrecorded breaches. This omission might be less significant if the researchers had not made the unjustified conclusion that a lack of recorded breaches meant the offenders had desisted from ASB. The report also involved no consideration of other factors such as maturation or other personal or social factors that may have been involved in desistence from ASB. Consequently, in all those cases where there was no record of a formal breach, it was *assumed* that it was the intervention alone that was effective. Thus, the claims made concerning the effectiveness of ASB interventions and ASBOs in particular must be treated with extreme caution. Also, claims about the effectiveness of different interventions – warning letters, Acceptable Behaviour Contracts and ASBOs that have been issued in different circumstances, to different types of offenders, for offences involving different degrees of seriousness – are not justified. Thus, although the research is relatively large scale and almost certainly a well-funded piece of work, it provides very little useful information on 'what works' and, most importantly, why and how it might work. Moreover, its conclusion that the government should develop more preventive measures does not follow from its own analysis. Indeed, some might think it ironic that an organisation that spends most of its time critically examining the cost effectiveness of other organisations should produce a research report of so little value.

A more informative piece of research has been carried out for the Youth Justice Board examining the case files of 137 young people from 10 sample areas who had received an ASBO from January 2004 to January 2005. The study also involved interviews with 59 key professionals, 45 young people and 22 parents of young people who have been given an ASBO (Solanki et al, 2006). The research found that just over three quarters of the sample had a previous criminal conviction. Interestingly, it noted that only one in five of the females who received an ASBO had a previous criminal conviction. In line with other research, it noted that only one in five of the young people who had received an ASBO lived in households with both of their birth parents, while almost half live in lone-parent households.

The study drew attention to the limited participation of Youth Offending Teams (YOTs) in the process of issuing an ASBO. Most workers complained that they were often not informed about cases until they were about to go to court or they heard from the young person concerned. This observation conveys a strong message about the limits of interagency working in ASBO cases. The study also points out that the increased use of CRASBOs also serves to undermine the case conferencing and interagency approach to the process of applying for ASBOs.

The research also highlights the considerable variation in the use of ASBOs in different areas and variations in the duration of orders, with some areas routinely issuing ASBOs for a two-year period and other making orders for five years of more. The report states that some of the practitioners interviewed felt that, rather than being tailored to the needs of the offender, conditions attached to ASBOs were often 'formulaic'. The practitioners interviewed, particularly the YOT workers, indicated that ASBOs could be extremely disruptive to the lives of young people and that conditions that involved geographical exclusions and non-association were unreasonable and in some cases counterproductive.

Interviews with magistrates and police officers revealed that applications for orders were rarely challenged and rejected. Indeed, it seemed to be assumed by the courts that if an order had been brought, all other avenues had been exhausted. By the same token, little consideration was given by the courts to exploring alternative sanctions. Approximately half of the young people in the sample had returned to court for failure to comply with their order, with the majority breaching on one or more occasions. The young people who received the ASBOs felt that the conditions were often unreasonable, while some did not have a clear understanding of the conditions specified in the order.

The report calls for greater involvement of YOTs in the decision-making process as well as regular reviews of ASBOs. It also suggests that the number and range of prohibitions involved in ASBOs should be reviewed and, in particular, that conditions involving geographical exclusion and non-association should not routinely be used for young people who, it is argued, need to spend time with their friends and have access to public space.

Despite the perceived limitations in the use of ASBOs, the study did find a relatively high degree of support for ASBOs, particularly in relation to the protection of vulnerable communities. However, the authors were concerned that ASBOs and other sanctions used to tackle ASB could result in a 'double-track' approach to youth justice, while the introduction of these new sanctions have, they suggest, considerable 'net-widening' potential.

Most of these reports were carried out concurrently with the research by the current authors and tended to examine a similar range of issues. However, each report provides a different focus and a different methodology. It is anticipated that this report will be read in conjunction with these other studies in order to build up a more comprehensive conceptual and methodological appreciation of the issues involved.

Research aims and methods

The three principal aims of the research were to examine the following:

- the impact of ASBOs on offenders;
- the perceived effectiveness of ASBOs among the agencies involved in their use;
- the views of victims and complainants who have either been personally subjected to anti-social behaviour or who live or work in areas experiencing anti-social behaviour.

The impact of ASBOs on different types of offenders was one of the primary aims of the research. It was anticipated that ASBOs, like other sanctions, would have a differential effect on different types of offenders in different situations and contexts and one of the main objectives was to examine this issue by engaging in detailed interviews with a range of offenders.

The second aim included an exploration of the decision-making processes used by agency staff involved in the use of ASBOs. It is particularly important to understand this, as the perceived effectiveness of ASBOs may be a function of the types of offenders and behaviours for which ASBOs are considered suitable. Thus, the criterion of selection requires examination.

Third, the experiences of complainants, victims and selected residents' groups were examined in order to find out about their respective views on the impact of ASBOs and to assess the degree to which the deployment of ASBOs addressed their concerns.

The research was conducted in seven London boroughs, and one location in the Midlands. These areas were selected on the basis of accessibility and the willingness of agencies to cooperate with the study. Out of a total sample of 66 offenders, 38 were selected from records held by the local authority and the remainder were obtained using networking and snowballing strategies; these were used to gain quick access because of the short time frame of the research. Twenty-nine interviews were conducted with practitioners, including police, anti-social behaviour officers, community safety officers, housing officers, YOT members, probation officers and magistrates. Detailed interviews were conducted with representatives of the British Transport Police in order to broaden the range of cases in which ASBOs were issued. Fourteen interviews were conducted with witnesses/complainants and seven focus groups were organised. In all, 121 interviews and seven focus groups were conducted over a 10-week period from October to December 2005.

The research took a detailed, qualitative, case-study approach to examine the impact of ASBOs from the perspective of offenders, ASB practitioners, victims, complainants and communities affected by ASB. The research had five key elements:

- examination of relevant records and documentation produced for each ASBO case;
- detailed, semi-structured, face-to-face interviews with ASBO subjects examining attitudes, behaviour and patterns of offending;
- semi-structured interviews with ASB practitioners;
- semi-structured interviews with victims and complainants;
- focus groups with communities affected by anti-social behaviour.

Each of these data sources combined to create case studies that were examined for the following factors:

- the reasons why an ASBO was sought;
- the role and composition of agencies involved;
- the use of ASBOs in relation to different forms of anti-social behaviour;
- the ways in which the relevant legislation was interpreted and applied by agencies;
- the exploration of alternative measures;
- the views of agency representatives on the appropriateness and effectiveness of ASBOs;
- the experience of the victim/complainant;
- the satisfaction of the victim/complainant with the action of agencies and the effectiveness of the ASBO;

- the offending history and background of offenders served with ASBOs;
- the experience of being served with an ASBO;
- the impact of ASBOs on family, friends and lifestyle;
- the impact of ASBOs on offending and commitment to anti-social behaviour;
- the views of members of the community on the role and value of ASBOs.

Offender sample

The offender sample included a slightly higher number of young people than exists in the total across England and Wales, with 44% under 18 years and 26% under 16 (compared with 50% and 33% respectively in England and Wales). Twenty per cent of the offenders interviewed were female (compared with 13% of the total in England and Wales). Sixty per cent of the sample classed themselves as White British, and 11% as mixed White and Black Caribbean. Of the 66 offenders interviewed, 30 had been issued with a full ASBO and 34 had been issued with a post-conviction ASBO.

Each interview was coded by the researchers according to the 'trigger' behaviours that precipitated the ASBO. These 'trigger' offences included ticket touting (seven), violent acts (seven), begging (three), criminal damage/graffiti (four), neighbour nuisance (10), prostitution (one), repeated criminal behaviour (11), substance misuse (10) and youth disorder (13).

Data analysis

The data obtained through these methods were analysed using N-Vivo and simple quantitative analyses such as t-tests and contingency tables.

Methodological qualifications

In some of the boroughs surveyed, the case files for different offenders were not always available. Also, it became evident that an increasing percentage of those receiving ASBOs were given ASBOs on conviction and therefore were not subject to the case-conferencing process. Consequently, comprehensive case files were only available for a limited number of the offenders included in the sample.

Due to the small non-random sample, the findings of this study should be considered as exploratory rather than representative of the entire population of ASBO subjects. In addition, the methods used to access interviewees may also have resulted in sample bias favouring those who were contactable by letter or telephone. Also, several offenders were interviewed in prison, which will give a bias towards those who have breached their order, or are more serious and persistent offenders.

2

Views from agencies

Introduction

The research looked at the operation, views and experiences of the relevant agencies in selecting and processing Anti-Social Behaviour Order (ASBO) cases. Its aim was to identify both the conceptual and practical issues that have arisen in different locations and in different agencies.

The findings are summarised under the following headings:

- Variations in attitudes and experience in different boroughs
- Interagency partnership and cooperation
- Criteria for selecting and processing cases
- The problem of definition
- The shift from ASBOs to CRASBOs
- Formulating the conditions for ASBOs
- The provision of support and welfare services
- The use of ASBOs in relation to ABCs and Parenting Orders
- Breaches and enforcement

Variations in attitudes and experience in different boroughs

Interviews with relevant staff were conducted in eight local authorities. Considerable differences were found in the different boroughs in relation to:

- the number of staff involved in dealing with anti-social behaviour;
- the number of ASBOs issued; and
- the types of offences for which ASBOs were deployed.

The size of the Anti-Social Behaviour Unit in each borough was taken by the researchers as an indicator of how seriously anti-social behaviour and ASBOs were viewed in each location. The variation may, however, also reflect the level and nature of anti-social behaviour in each locality. Different boroughs adopted different strategies to deal with anti-social behaviour and frequently used other measures, apart from ASBOs, to respond to different forms of anti-social behaviour. Table 2.1 below provides an indication of the numbers of staff in the eight boroughs surveyed in the anti-social behaviour (ASB) team and the number of ASBOs issued up to December 2005.

In general, there was an identifiable division between those agencies that advocated the use of ASBOs – the police, the Anti-Social Behaviour Unit, housing department

Table 2.1: Numbers of ASB staff and ASBOs, by borough

Borough	Number of staff	Number of ASBOs
Barking and Dagenham	4	23
Brent	6	24
Islington	7	14
Lambeth	1	38*
Leicester	6	24
Redbridge	8	23
Southwark	6	51
Westminster	5	40

* While the fieldwork for this project was being undertaken, Lambeth had yet to collate detailed information on the number of ASBOs and CRASOs in the borough. This figure, therefore, is an estimate.

and magistrates – and the various welfare and support agencies – the Youth Offending Teams (YOTs), probation, social services and others – who were more sceptical about their use. It was evident that these groups had oppositional perspectives, with the advocates seeing ASBOs mainly as a preventive sanction and the sceptics seeing it essentially as a mode of enforcement (see Table 2.2) Although there are considerable differences of perspective, it did not mean that these agencies were not able to work together and in a certain number of cases to agree on the use of ASBOs.

Table 2.2: Alternative views on the role and function of ASBOs by different agencies

Item	Advocates	Sceptics
Objective of sanction	Prevention	Enforcement
Target group	Community/ neighbourhoods	Offenders/clients
Effect of sanction	Social cohesion	Social exclusion
Motivation of offender	Lack of respect/ consideration	Deprivation/ vulnerability

The police, in particular, were generally supportive of the use of ASBOs, although some pointed to the problems of gathering sufficient evidence and the time delays involved. One police officer saw ASBOs as a useful sanction for dealing with groups of rowdy young people:

> 'What I can say generally is that a particular area is quieter since we have been targeting the youths' behaviour and part of that is just using ASBOs.... Generally it has had an impact by helping to take out some of the main players in that group of kids.'

A similar view was expressed by a representative of the British Transport Police, who felt that ASBOs had been very effective in reducing the number of ticket touts operating in stations, although in this officer's opinion they did not work for all types of offenders:

> 'A lot have been given a 10-year ASBO and they just disappear. I don't think that ASBOs work for kids on council estates – they're not geared for that, but drug addicts here – it works.'

Most of the agency representatives interviewed appeared more comfortable about ASBOs when they were used as a last resort after all other options had been tried and tested. A typical comment on the use of ASBOs as a last resort was given by a member of an anti-social behaviour team:

> 'I think ASBOs have to be a last resort for us, to be honest. I think that part of me feels that if you've got to the ASBO stage, then perhaps you have failed somewhere along the way but accepting that there are some people where you will have to go to the last resort because they are not going to respond otherwise.'

Some respondents believed that this was what they were required to do, although the recent Home Office guidelines on the use of ASBOs say explicitly that they do not need to be used as a last resort. Even among those who wanted to use ASBOs as a last resort, there were a number of reasons why this objective was not pursued. These included:

- pragmatic considerations, such as the perceived seriousness, persistence or danger posed by specific offenders;
- the perceived need to provide powerful interventions and protect the community;
- limited participation in the process by certain welfare and support agencies, which in some cases meant that the available range of options could not be fully explored.

In most of the boroughs, some of the main welfare and support agencies either did not participate in the case conferences or felt that they were peripheral members and that the 'core group' driving the process forward was the police, the housing department and the Anti-Social Behaviour Unit. As they saw it, their role was to provide relevant evidence rather than to engage in a detailed discussion of what services could and should be made available. As one youth worker put it:

> 'What's happening is that a lot of ASBOs are being made without social services interventions, without YOT knowledge and so forth. So prohibitions are often sort of like irrelevant or too stringent or basically you are just setting the kids up to fail.'

As one care worker explained, there was tension between cooperating with the police in relation to gathering evidence for ASBOs, and keeping faith with clients:

'They convened these multi-agency meetings … and we had the police and us and a few other agencies – if they turned up – to try to address the individuals who were seen regularly but then the monitoring that went on in those meetings gradually became a kind of tick-list of loads of people getting ASBOs.… We weren't contributing figures to these meetings. We were contributing kind of information about people's support needs.'

Interagency partnership and cooperation

All but one borough had an Anti-Social Behaviour Unit, although the size of these units varied considerably between one and eight staff. All the boroughs examined used some form of interagency cooperation and a 'case conference' model for considering different offenders for an ASBO. There were considerable differences in the agencies involved and the role that they played in each borough. Generally, the approach adopted in processing cases tended to involve two or three key agencies working closely with the police. In some boroughs, the system of processing cases was disorganised, with infrequent meetings, and there were problems of coordination and data gathering. Other boroughs reported ongoing tensions between the police and the local authority over the regulation of ASB and particularly over the processing of ASBOs.

Ongoing tensions within partnerships did not, however, prevent people from working together and agreeing on interventions. The situation in most of the boroughs was reflected in the experience of one anti-social behaviour team member:

'I've only been to a couple of ASBO case conferences but they are good meetings. There might be tension between the YOT and other partners, but generally I've always thought that at the end of the day there tends to be agreement on the way forward and I've never known a real breakdown. It's taken a while to build up that sort of trust because obviously, as you can imagine, people that are working with young people may well have a resistance and see us as wanting to criminalise young people.'

Although the police were generally supportive of anti-social behaviour policies and the use of ASBOs, they also expressed the following concerns:

- The anti-social behaviour agenda was seen to be council-led, with the police playing a limited role in setting priorities but being expected to play a major role in processing and enforcing ASBOs.
- The police were being called on to gather evidence and process cases they felt were extremely time-consuming.

- Controlling anti-social behaviour was not seen as proper police work and distracted them from concentrating on realising their crime targets.
- Securing ASBOs was seen as taking too long and creating tensions with the public who wanted a rapid response.

The deployment of ASBOs was seen by the different agencies involved to blur lines of responsibility, to erode the distinction between prevention and enforcement, and generally to create new tensions between partners. Directly related to these tensions is the problem of gathering and coordinating good-quality information from the relevant agencies. Some agencies are reluctant to provide information on their clients and this can delay the processing of cases or alternatively affect the nature and quality of evidence presented in court.

Criteria for selecting and processing cases

The criteria for selecting and processing cases is a critical component in evaluating the effectiveness of ASBOs, since their success or failure, in part, is a function of the type of person selected. There appeared to be a number of routes that lead offenders to be considered for an ASBO. These include:

- the type of behaviour;
- the level and nature of public complaints;
- the perceived impact on the community;
- the persistence of the behaviour concerned;
- the exhaustion of other options;
- breaching or non-compliance with Acceptable Behaviour Contracts (ABCs).

It was found that cases referred to the Anti-Social Behaviour Unit would normally be subject to a number of tests:

- Has the behaviour been persistent and continuous for at least two months prior to the initiation of the order?
- Have other measures been tried and appear not to have worked?
- Is there sufficient credible evidence?
- Is the anti-social behaviour detrimental to a number of members of the community, not just one or two individuals?

In some cases, additional criteria are employed, such as whether it falls within local priorities for the Crime and Disorder Reduction Partnership. The process of selection in one borough was summarised in the following terms by an anti-social behaviour coordinator:

'The use of ASBOs is really about risk assessment and it is about the persistence of offending. What we would say is, "What is the risk to the victims?", "What is the risk to witnesses?", "What is the risk to the community?". And if it is high risk, then what we might say is that we need to move straight towards an ASBO rather than any other intervention…. There will be other cases that will be more about persistence with the perpetrator or where we might have issued warnings or have gone through an ABC process that hasn't worked.'

Once the decision has been taken in a case conference to apply for an ASBO, normally the anti-social behaviour coordinator, in conjunction with the police, sets about gathering the necessary information and producing impact statements. Gathering evidence can, however, be a time-consuming operation. As one police officer seconded to an Anti-Social Behaviour Unit pointed out, collecting good-quality evidence involves a considerable amount of research and a great deal of time. He explained:

'And the kind of intrinsic difficulty with all these cases is that there are many sources of evidence…. So it is not just a question of looking at someone's previous convictions or a complaint made against a neighbour…. The difficulty is that out of all the information and intelligence that there might be there is very little that you can use. In one case of a youth offender there was over 300 intelligence reports but there was only eight that had credible evidence that you could use to support an application. But somebody still had to trawl through the 300 reports and whittle them down to 50, whittle them down to eight, and that is what people just do not have the ability and time to do.'

In some case files we examined, the offending histories were listed. The evidence that was presented in court was largely dependent on the information that was generated between the time when the offender was placed on the ASBO register and the date they appeared in court. This evidence, which was frequently police-generated through stops and surveillance, was then presented in court together with the offending history of the suspect, including a number of spent convictions. The implication of this finding is that a significant amount of the evidence presented in court can involve incidents that have taken place after the ASBO has been sought and those in which no arrest or other formal action has taken place. As one YOT manager explained:

'There are certain kids … who are going to be targeted because the police think that they are a nuisance. We have a lot of kids who get quite a lot of Stops and they go to court. That's why I like to be involved.'

In establishing the criteria for proceeding with an ASBO, the agencies concerned are sensitive to the requirements and attitudes of magistrates. Thus in one case, an application for an ASBO against a noisy neighbour was rejected on the grounds that other measures could have been used, such as seizing the equipment used for making the noise. We know little, however, about the criteria that different magistrates apply in granting orders and the attitudes of magistrates towards the use of ASBOs in general.

We did, however, interview four magistrates, one of whom pointed out that children being served ASBOs are dealt with in the adult court. He clearly felt that this was inappropriate, but because the youth court does not have a civil jurisdiction there is no option but to hear cases of young people in an adult court where agencies such as the YOT are not present.

The problem of definition

Agency staff repeatedly identified the problems that exist with the definition of anti-social behaviour. The lack of an adequate definition created conceptual problems regarding the type of behaviour that should be targeted and practical problems about which agencies should take responsibility for developing interventions.

A number of police officers were concerned with the overlap between activities that were defined as anti-social behaviour but were in fact criminal offences – in some cases quite serious ones. Anti-social behaviour can include acts of violence, robbery and theft, all of which are widely considered to be mainstream crimes.

As one police officer pointed out, the overlap and indeed the duplication between ASB and crime leads not only to the possibility of double counting but can cause confusions in practice in relation to roles and responsibilities of the different agencies involved. He stated:

> 'If people commit a criminal offence, it is a matter for the police to prosecute them and take them to the courts and it is a matter for the courts to prosecute them on the basis of those events. ASBOs are used as a back-door means by the police to persuade the council that it is the council's responsibility that kids have broken windows etc. Well, I think that it is a bit of a con perpetrated by the police on councils, actually.'

This quotation captures the ambivalence of some of the police officers we interviewed who, on the one hand, wanted what they considered to be crimes to be dealt with by the police and the criminal courts, and, on the other hand, saw ASBOs as way of transferring responsibility for dealing with relatively minor but persistence offenders on to the council.

Another form of frustration reported by agency representatives was the desire by some members of the community to deal with all forms of annoying behaviour by issuing an ASBO. One senior policy officer, for example, complained that the lack of precision in the definition of anti-social behaviour and a lack of clear guidelines on the types of behaviour that ASBOs should be used for resulted in residents demanding

that ASBOs be used to deal with all forms of behaviour they found irritating or felt were undesirable. Thus, in commenting on a recent meeting with residents, this council official stated:

> 'I go to a resident group meeting and people say to me, "Those kids ride their bicycles around the car park of the estate" and I say, "Do they knock you over? Do they abuse you verbally? Do they harass you? Are they banging on cars? Are they running over smaller children? Do they have anywhere else to ride their bicycles?". To me, that's not anti-social.'

The Home Office (2004) publication *Defining and Measuring Anti Social Behaviour* suggests that the decision about what to include as anti-social behaviour should lie with practitioners after gathering evidence of anti-social behaviour in their area (which presupposes that they know what anti-social behaviour is), while the Home Affairs Committee (2005) noted that the standard definitions of ASB are 'capable of being interpreted differently by different people' (p 16) and suggested that the decision about what constitutes ASB should be decided locally with local residents having their say. However, it was clear in the interviews with practitioners that that they were, in some cases at least, sceptical of the views of local residents, as the quotation above exemplifies, while, as we shall see in the chapter below on community responses, residents felt that their concerns were not always taken seriously by practitioners.

A number of respondents felt that anti-social behaviour was originally presented as involving 'neighbours from hell' and rowdy gangs of youngsters, but that in practice the vagueness of the definition of anti-social behaviour had allowed interventions to be directed at a wide range of activities, while giving the authorities considerable discretion in deciding which forms of behaviour and what groups of people they wanted to target.

The shift from ASBOs to CRASBOs

It became apparent in examining case files that the number of Anti-Social Behaviour Orders on Conviction (CRASBOs) issued has been increasing steadily over the past two years, such that in five out of eight boroughs where we interviewed agency staff, the number of CRASBOs issued has outstripped the number of stand-alone ASBOs (see Table 2.3 below). Data provided by the British Transport Police revealed that, out of 171 ASBOs issued up to December 2005, 160 were CRASBOs.

The obvious attraction to practitioners of CRASBOs is that they are quicker and less costly than processing stand-alone ASBOs. They also have a high degree of certainty once a conviction has been achieved. As one policy officer explained, either a CRASBO can be used in cases where an ASBO is under consideration and the offender is due to appear in court in the near future or where the pattern and history of offending is such that an ASBO is deemed to be appropriate. As long as the

Table 2.3: Numbers of ASBOs and CRASBOs issued in each borough, 2002-05

Borough	ASBOs	CRASBOs	Total
Barking and Dagenham	13	10	23
Brent	3	21	24
Islington	4	10	14
Lambeth	n/a	n/a	38*
Leicester	24	0	24
Redbridge	7	16	23
Southwark	50	1	51
Westminster	11	29	40

* While the fieldwork for this project was being undertaken, Lambeth had yet to collate detailed information on the number of ASBOs and CRASBOs in the borough. This figure, therefore, is an estimate.

paperwork is ready and the necessary evidence is available, a CRASBO can be sought at this point, saving time and effort. Alternatively:

'If you've got someone who is, say, a prolific burglar who also happens to be an anti-social general pain in the arse to everybody that they come across ... so you'd take an ASBO on them – but their burglary is also an issue – then that would be ideal to have a post-conviction ASBO.'

Cases were reported, however, in which offenders claimed that they were not aware that a CRASBO might be sought and were surprised when this additional sanction was added to their original sentence. Our data would also suggest, despite low numbers, that ASBOs are more likely to be served on a younger population, while CRASBOs are more likely to be issued to older, more serious, offenders, as Figure 2.1 indicates:

There are a number of issues that were highlighted in the research in relation to the growing use of CRASBOs:

- Formal procedures, such as case conferencing, by which the suitability of an ASBO is discussed and agreed by key agencies, are sidestepped.
- As a result, key agencies may be unaware of the fact that a CRASBO is being served. This was found to lead to tensions and suspicions and may serve to undermine interagency cooperation.
- Issues are raised regarding the imposition of a 'second sentence' and the nature of sentencing policy in relation to issues of proportionality, rights and due process.
- The use of CRASBOs has implications for the possibility of revoking the ASBO. Because CRASBOs are tied to a conviction the likelihood of revoking them is less than for a stand-alone ASBO.

Figure 2.1: ASBOs and CRASBOs issued by age of offender interviewed (n=66)

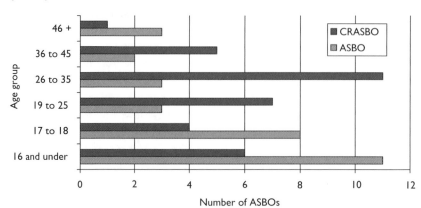

- There is little likelihood that CRASBOs will be linked to the provision of care and support strategies for offenders and therefore they may be more likely to be breached.
- CRASBOs may lose much of their preventive powers and are seen mainly as a form of punishment.
- The use of ASBOs on conviction makes it much more difficult to assess the effectiveness and impact of ASBOs, since they are tied to other types of sentence.

One magistrate expressed a positive view on the use of CRASBOs and felt that they were more likely to be effective because they represented an additional or ancillary sentence. He felt that running an ASBO alongside a Supervision Order, for example, was likely to increase its effectiveness by giving additional support and formal contact with the person concerned.

On the other hand, considerable antipathy was expressed by a number of community safety officers and anti-social behaviour coordinators in relation to the use of CRASBOs. Some found it difficult to see why an ASBO should be added to the criminal sanction, since prior to the development of ASBOs the sentences given out at court were generally seen to be adequate. As one community safety manager put it:

> 'I am still not sure why we have CRASBOs, since enforcement of them is more difficult. Courts can use them off their own bat. What is it supposed to do?.... The police have their own logic, which I fail to understand most of the time. There is an alignment with the partnership, but outside the partnership the police are led by different imperatives.'

Formulating the conditions for ASBOs

One of the most frequently cited limitations of ASBOs by agency representatives was the conditions attached to many orders. It was felt, even by those who strongly supported the use of ASBOs, that the formulation of conditions was often inadequate. In some cases, the conditions imposed were seen as extreme. As one police officer who had been seconded to an Anti-Social Behaviour Unit pointed out:

> 'The broader they are the less effective they are. I think that we have lost the plot a little bit with multi-conditions. The most effective ones are where we are taking [a] one or two conditions approach. Where the ASBO covers all of England and Wales who is going to enforce that? Some conditions say in effect, "Don't break the law", but if they break the law they will be charged for committing a criminal offence – not for breaching the ASBO.'

In general, the comments from practitioners suggested that, in a significant number of cases, the conditions imposed tended to be:

* inappropriate;
* excessive;
* impractical; and
* unenforceable.

These deficiencies tended to overlap and there was a widespread view that conditions are often poorly formulated and conceived. In the more extreme examples, which tend to get widely publicised, the credibility of ASBOs tends to be called into question. In the words of one anti-social behaviour manager:

> 'I mean, in some cases they are badly framed and they have some stupid conditions which I quite frankly would not want to put people in prison for breaching.'

However, many of the practitioners who expressed reservations about the nature of the conditions specified in ASBOs were themselves more or less directly involved in processing ASBOs and agreeing to the conditions included in the orders. It would seem, therefore, that those who made these critical observations were either fairly removed from the process of formulating conditions in their borough or they were making reference to cases they had come across in other boroughs. It may also be the case that many of those involved in processing ASBOs are on a steep learning curve and have come to identify conditions that have been included in the past as inappropriate, possibly because they have been consistently breached or because they have come realise that the way that the conditions have been formulated make them extremely difficult to enforce.

Particular issues arose around the ASBO conditions given to young people:

- an order with a two-year minimum duration was considered inappropriate, since young people were seen to be in period of rapid change and maturation;
- conditions preventing association with other young people in a group are impractical and detrimental to social development by intensifying their marginalised status, thereby increasing their commitment to anti-social behaviour.

One magistrate also expressed some scepticism about the possibility of changing the behaviour of young people by giving them a set of prohibitions linked to the threat of imprisonment, advocating instead a more incremental and structured approach (see Solanki et al, 2006).

The provision of support and welfare services

One community safety manager expressed the view that the recipients of ASBOs in his borough could be divided into roughly three groups – 'the mad, the sad and the bad'. By this, he was suggesting that he believed that a significant proportion of those given ASBOs either suffer from some form of mental illness or psychological problem or have a history of drug and alcohol abuse, or alternatively they have an established criminal career. The majority of young people in our sample include those, for example, who are referred to as NEETs (Not in Education, Employment or Training) and a significant percentage have been subject to some form of social exclusion (see Chapter 3).

If it is the case that not all of the options are in fact 'exhausted' before an ASBO is applied, there is an opportunity once an offender is placed on the ASBO register to mobilise support services. However, the interviews with agency representatives revealed that there was little evidence in most boroughs of any systematic strategy of engaging with offenders who had been placed on the ASBO register or who had been served with an ASBO. We found a number of examples of specific individuals and agencies that had a firm commitment to providing support to those receiving ASBOs, but the degree of commitment varied considerably in different locations.

There was some concern among agency representatives in the London area that as the number of ASBOs issued increased, some boroughs, particularly those that resort to using ASBOs most frequently, could engage in a deliberate process of displacement and of using ASBOs as a way of 'washing their hands' of troublesome people. At the same time, those neighbouring boroughs that are the likely recipients of these 'outcasts' may themselves be encouraged to engage in similar strategies in the future, in order not to be overwhelmed with 'problem populations'.

The patchy and inconsistent provision of services at different stages of the process in some boroughs is unfortunate because a number of respondents felt strongly that it was only when an ASBO or the threat of an ASBO was linked to positive and supportive interventions that they had a real possibility of changing offenders' attitudes and behaviour.

One police officer put forward this view when discussing a recent case involving a young person:

> 'An ASBO in isolation, an ASBO without the YOT putting in extra resources, would have been breached on a daily basis. The fundamental thing about them is that they are not behavioural tools. They are not interventions that will impact upon someone's behaviour. They are a boundary and if they decide to go over that they will be arrested, but they are not a positive intervention. They are a bit negative. It's like a "do not."'

In the Home Office guidelines (Home Office, 2005), it is clear that ASBOs are meant not to be used as a purely negative and exclusionary sanction, but rather to be linked to the mobilisation of appropriate services. The available evidence suggests that the provision of such services in relation to the use of ASBOs is generally inadequate. Moreover, in some boroughs, there was evidence that ASBOs were being sought in cases in which the welfare and support agencies had either given up on individuals or were unable or unwilling to help them any more. Thus, one police officer reported that "the care agencies would actually be suggesting to us people to look at for ASBOs because they knew they couldn't help them".

The case study below on street drinkers identifies some of the problems and complexities associated with serving ASBOs on marginalised groups. In this case, the Anti-Social Behaviour Unit saw the initiative as a success in that it reduced the visibility of street drinking and dispersed the individuals involved. However, there was evidence of geographical displacement and some of the street drinkers were sent to prison for breaching the conditions of their orders (see Young et al, 2006). Based on detailed interviews with a number of different practitioners in the borough, the case study indicates some of the processes involved in addressing the issue of street drinking and responding to the complaints of members of the community.

Street drinking: a case study

The situation: In this borough, between 20 and 30 street drinkers met regularly in a particular location, causing nuisance and blocking the streets. There were also reports of fights and disturbances, and on some occasions, street drinkers urinating on the pavement. Mounting complaints from local residents and shopkeepers put pressure on the local council to take action.

The intervention: The local day centre, which conducted outreach work with this group, provided meals and other amenities, and ran a 'wet centre' two days a week where the drinkers could meet together away from the street.

This was effective on the days it operated, but the funding for it was removed in the autumn of 2005. At the same time as funding ceased, the council and police started to gather evidence for imposing ABCs and ASBOs on this group. The centre staff did not feel that ABCs and ASBOs were appropriate for this group, and favoured a street drinking ban that had been applied in neighbouring boroughs to good effect. This involved a more informal, low-key form of policing in which street drinkers could be dispersed and their drink confiscated. The council and police favoured ABCs and ASBOs, and the manager of the day centre felt they were also under pressure to support these sanctions and to meet targets for the borough. The police attempted to persuade the day-centre staff to supply evidence for the ASBOs, but they were reluctant to cooperate, except that there were, in the manager's view, thinly veiled threats made about the future funding of the day centre if he did not cooperate.

The impact: The initial impact was that the day centre lost the trust of many of its clients because the staff were seen to be working with the police against them. The threat of impending ASBOs encouraged some of the more casual drinkers and 'hangers-on' to move out of the area and to drink elsewhere. Some were served with ABCs, which in most cases persuaded the drinkers to find other locations to drink, while four 'hardcore drinkers' were given ASBOs. Two breached the ASBOs and were given short prison sentences. Not all the ASBOs included forms of geographical exclusion because the magistrate had rejected this condition in some cases. The effect on the community has been fairly positive in as much as it has dispersed the street drinking group, although a few now drink in the local park.

An assessment: In the opinion of some of the practitioners involved, the majority of these street drinkers suffer from forms of mental illness or personality disorders, and it was felt by certain respondents that ASBOs were more appropriate for dealing with 'neighbours from hell' rather than what were seen as vulnerable groups. The future of funding of the day centre is reported to be uncertain and it was felt by those who ran the day centre that funding was being increasingly directed towards enforcement rather than care.

The police and the anti-social behaviour team hailed the intervention as a significant success and felt that they had been effective in breaking up the 'hard-core' group by issuing ASBOs. Some practitioners, particularly the police, felt that ASBOs were necessary to have an impact on the situation and suggested that serving an ASBO on some of the more serious and persistent offenders could be effective in persuading them to change their ways and maybe to receive some support and welfare services, either in the community or in prison.

The use of ASBOs in relation to ABCs and Parenting Orders

Acceptable Behaviour Contracts

Acceptable Behaviour Contracts are written agreements between a person and the local housing office or Registered Social Landlord and the local police. The person agrees not to carry out a series of identifiable behaviours that have been defined as anti-social. The contracts were initially aimed at young people aged between 10 and 18 years of age, but are now used for adults as well.

There was considerable support among agency representatives for the use of ABCs, particularly among those under 16, who were seen as being responsive and approachable. One police officer pointed out that ABCs were the preferred option for young offenders in his borough as they are easier to process than ASBOs and were seen to be more effective in changing behaviour. He suggested that this was because ABCs involved some engagement with the young person and their family and pointed out that research that had been carried out in the borough found that over 80% of those served with ABCs did not reoffend within the first six months of the contract. As in other boroughs, the use of ABCs was seen to be effective and as a consequence they were frequently used as an alternative to ASBOs, often to good effect.

ABCs involve a contractual base that allows discussion with the offenders about taking responsibility for their actions. In contrast to the ASBO, which, it was suggested is sometimes seen by offenders as a constraining sanction, the ABC afforded offenders the opportunity of keeping out of trouble and avoiding unwanted pressures to misbehave.

Both an ABC and an ASBO can serve as a 'wake-up call' for offenders. However, the ABC sets in motion various options, while the ASBO is seen to limit options and further marginalise offenders. There was general feeling among a number of respondents that, as a rule, ABCs tended to be used for more minor but persistent offenders, while ASBOs were more usually used in relation to more serious offences and older offenders. In some boroughs, there appeared to be an unwritten rule that ASBOs would only be considered for young people if they had previously been given an ABC that they had breached. As one youth worker stated:

> 'We haven't, as yet, supported any kid getting an ASBO that hasn't been through the ABC process, or been offered it.'

Parenting Orders

Parenting Orders can be given to the parents/carers of young people who offend or truant, or who have received a Child Safety Order or an Anti-Social Behaviour Order. It lasts for three months but can be extended to 12 months. A parent/carer who receives a Parenting Order is required to attend counselling and guidance sessions. Other conditions may be attached to the order, such as ensuring that the child does not visit a particular place unsupervised or is at home at set times. A failure to fulfil the conditions can be treated as a criminal offence and the parent/carer can be prosecuted.

In general, there was limited awareness among agency respondents of the relationship between ASBOs and other sanctions to deal with anti-social behaviour. In one borough, the anti-social behaviour coordinator said that he was planning to use Parenting Orders in preference to ASBOs, but there was a limited awareness of how sanctions might be usefully combined.

In one case where an ASBO was linked to a Parenting Order, it appeared to be effective. In this case, at the same time that a teenager was given an ASBO, his mother, who was very concerned about his behaviour and blamed herself, applied for a Parenting Order. These two orders running simultaneously served to reinforce each other and the teenager changed his ways and eventually went to college. Interestingly in this case, as in other similar cases, there was evidence of a very supportive mother who took on some of the responsibility and worked with her child to encourage a positive change in behaviour.

Some parents either did not feel responsible for their children's behaviour or else were opposed to them receiving ASBOs. A number of agency representatives expressed the view that some parents of young people given ASBOs welcomed the intervention because they felt that their children were getting out of control and that in some cases that the ASBO mobilised peer pressure, which was seen to be effective in modifying the attitudes of these young people.

Breaches and enforcement

The majority of local authority representatives admitted that they kept only patchy records of the number and types of breaches that occurred if records were kept at all. Where there were records, it was apparent that many orders had been breached on a number of occasions and it was not unusual to find an order breached five or six times. Only two local authorities had regular monitoring meetings that covered breaches. Consequently, in most boroughs there was only anecdotal information on the number and type of breaches. One anti-social behaviour coordinator admitted that:

'There is no monitoring of the behaviour of those with Anti-Social Behaviour Orders. If information comes to light from residents' groups, police or other agencies, the anti-social behaviour team will take action. Because of the lack of monitoring, there is no record of breaches. It is believed that breaching the exclusion area is the most common breach, but that is anecdotal and not statistical. Applications for the removal of an ASBO are not made by the team – they are just left to run their course.'

Reports of breaches tend to come from police neighbourhood teams, residents and community groups. Some practitioners felt that the courts were not firm enough in dealing with breaches and that this sent out a message that breaches were being condoned. There were some concerns expressed about the areas of exclusion stipulated in many cases. In cases in which the area of exclusion was extensive, it was more difficult to enforce the ASBO. For many offenders, the area in which they operated tended to be fairly circumscribed. Some local authorities, however, frequently applied for a wide area of exclusion. In some cases, this restricted access to important services, family members and friends.

In one borough that kept reasonably detailed information on breaches, it was found that all but one of the offenders given an ASBO had breached the order, with an average number of 2.6 breaches per individual. Some of these breaches resulted in the imposition of various penalties, including Supervision Orders, Detention and Training Orders and Community Rehabilitation Orders. However, not all breaches were enforced or resulted in court action. In most boroughs surveyed, the response to breaches appeared relatively inconsistent. As one police officer stated:

'Breaches of ASBOs are dealt with haphazardly, and one magistrate will do one thing and the next magistrate sitting in the next court in the same building would do something completely different and I think that is inexcusable.... I've been to court many times with ASBOs over the past couple of years and it is absolutely disgusting to see magistrates just be wishy-washy and didn't care what the information was. Their sentencing policy is totally erratic.'

It was emphasised by some respondents that from their perspective a breach was not necessarily a sign of failure. Where the primary purpose of the ASBO is seen to be the protection of the community, ASBOs, although breached, may still act to reduce the level of anti-social behaviour and give relief to blighted neighbourhoods. Some respondents expressed the view that it was only after individuals had been given a fine or some other sanction as a consequence of breaching the order that the seriousness and reality of the order became fully apparent. An officer from the British Transport Police put it in the following terms:

'The initial ASBO makes little difference. But after a few breaches they get the message. At first it's a £30 fine, which is rubbish. But then it gets harder.'

Although it was not possible to engage in a detailed examination of breaches because of the lack of available data, it was indicative in one borough that kept records that 80% of known breaches occurred within six months after receiving the ASBO.

These points raise a number of issues for consideration:

- the relation between the likelihood of breaches and the number and form of the conditions of the order;
- whether other measures could be developed alongside the imposition of ASBOs to reduce the probability of breaches;
- what the appropriate sanction should be for different types of breaches;
- whether ASBOs should be closely monitored in the first six months after they are issued.

The interviews with practitioners revealed that the following issues were particularly pertinent to ASBO breaches:

- Welfare and support agencies do not necessarily inform the police and other agencies when they become aware that a breach has occurred.
- Police in some boroughs felt that enforcement of the ASBO conditions and monitoring breaches was not their responsibility.
- There were difficulties in mobilising witnesses and persuading them to give evidence in court.

In sum, there exist a number of tensions and problems in the processing and implementation of ASBOs. A number of issues relating to the monitoring and evaluation of this sanction remain unresolved and there are uncertainties about the appropriate lines of responsibility.

3

The impact on offenders

Introduction

The research examined the impact of Anti-Social Behaviour Orders (ASBOs) on a range of offenders, particularly in relation to their propensity to engage in anti-social behaviour and future offending. The frequency with which orders were breached was also investigated, as well as the impact of the order on the offender's personal life, including their personal and family relationships. This chapter draws on the information gathered from the 38 completed cases and the 28 additional offender interviews that were undertaken.

Our findings are summarised under the following headings:

- Offending histories
- Social, personal and psychological histories
- Attitudes towards being given an ASBO
- Responses to the conditions of the order
- Impact of ASBOs on offenders
- Geographic and functional displacement
- Number and type of breaches
- Impact on personal, social and family life

Offending histories

The offending histories of those issued with stand-alone ASBOs were obtained through a review of the case files kept by the local Anti-Social Behaviour Units (ASBUs). The offending histories of those interviewed ranged from those with no previous criminal convictions to those with multiple convictions. A range of convictions was reported, from burglary to affray, criminal damage, shoplifting, hoax calls, robbery, soliciting, ticket touting, graffiti, actual bodily harm (ABH), grievous bodily harm (GBH), being drunk and disorderly, breach of the peace, motor vehicle offences and so on.

Table 3.1 is based on 38 cases in which there was access to case files. A quarter of those for whom this information was available had no previous convictions, with 60% having one or more previous conviction and at least 15% having more than five. Two fifths of the offenders reported having received other sanctions either prior to or in parallel with the ASBO. Of the orders issued, reported Supervision Orders were the most common, with one quarter reporting receiving this type of order.

Table 3.1: Number of pre-convictions (n=38)

Number of pre-convictions	Total
0	8
1	3
2	2
3	4
4	3
5	4
>10	5
Missing data	9
Total	38

In the entire interview sample (n=66), offences against the person constituted 42% of the total. Where no personal offence had been committed, just under half (47%) of offences involved theft or damage. Only 8% of cases solely involved drugs or disorder. These data indicate (however tentatively, given the sample size) that conventional forms of criminality rather than disorder were the main driver for orders.

Apart from criminal convictions, many of those on ASBOs also had numerous allegations included in their records that had not led to convictions. Some case files also contained entries drawn from other criminal justice system databases, such as the police call-out recording tool CADMIS (Command and Dispatch Management Information System) and the London-wide police research tool CRIMINT (criminal intelligence). Several of the young people reported that they had been listed as persistent and prolific offenders.

Social, personal and psychological histories

The social, personal and psychological histories of those who had received ASBOs were examined in order to provide a basis for the analysis of the types of factors that may influence the impact that an ASBO might have on an individual's anti-social behaviour, on their personal life and on their future prospects.

The offenders were from a diverse range of backgrounds, with approximately two fifths of those interviewed living in local authority housing. Nearly one fifth were living in hostels or other temporary accommodation, or were sleeping rough. Another fifth were still living with their parents. In line with previous research, it was found that a large number were unemployed or on sickness benefits and many had not obtained any educational qualifications or training (see Koffman, 2006).

Seven interviewees (11%) reported that they had been diagnosed with, or had received treatment for, some form of mental health and psychological issue, including depression, anxiety, attempted suicide, conduct disorder or attention deficit hyperactivity disorder (ADHD). Two of these seven indicated that they were currently taking prescription medication related to their condition.

While the qualitative nature of the research and small sample size limits what can be said about the relationship between an offender's social, personal and psychological history and their proclivity to continue to behave anti-socially, the researchers encountered a number of people (23%) who 'self-reported' past traumatic events, such as the suicide of a relative, sexual assault, homelessness, physical illness, self-harm or depression. Over two thirds reported having problems with alcohol or illegal drug dependency. Two fifths reported problems with alcohol, including one 17-year-old who was a registered alcoholic.[1]

Many young people reported living with parents or families that were violent, had psychological or drug problems, or were offenders themselves. Seven of the young people interviewed had been excluded from school, while two were persistent truants. Others in the sample came from supportive single- or two-parent families, some with extended families living in close proximity. One young person, who had been served with a five-year ASBO, had been given a pupil of the year award by his school. Another was the daughter of a local councillor.

Attitudes towards being given an ASBO

The attitudes of those who had been served with an ASBO ranged from anger and annoyance at one extreme to relief at the other. Table 3.2 shows the different attitudes reported during the interviews and provides an indication of the proportion of interviewees reporting each type of attitude. It should be noted that the responses provided by interviewees were not exclusive and in some cases interviewees reported multiple or contradictory reactions, while others reported none at all.

Two fifths of the interviewees felt that the ASBO was unfair, inappropriate or disproportionate in relation to the type of offence they had committed. Many of those who felt angry argued that in their opinion there were people committing more serious offences but receiving lesser punishments. Among this group, there were frequent claims that the evidence used to obtain the order was questionable

---

[1] In addition to this, the interviewers, who were experienced social researchers but who do not have medical or psychiatric qualifications, indicated a further 17% of interviewees where there could be possible underlying mental health or psychological conditions.

Table 3.2: Interviewees' attitudes to receiving an ASBO

Attitudes	%
Order seen as unfair, inappropriate or disproportionate	33
Anger/annoyance	14
Relief (for not being given a more severe sentence)	8
Order seen as a joke/stupid/weak sanction	8
Offender scared/fearful of consequences/daunted	6
Order seen as an erosion of rights and freedom of movement	5
Offender indifferent/not bothered	5
Order seen as fair and reasonable	4
Other	15

and in a few cases respondents denied committing the acts for which the ASBO had been given.

One of the more extreme responses to receiving an ASBO was provided by one prolific adult offender:

'It certainly turns you into a violent, angry young man and I've never been violent.... I am fucking fuming ... fucking fuming.'

A small number of respondents felt that the ASBO was overly punitive and had unfairly restricted their movements or ability to see family and friends. Such complaints were made most often about geographic conditions, non-association and curfews. Interviewees often reported breaching conditions they felt were unfair. As one persistent young offender put it:

'I can't see my family. Most don't live around here where I am boxed in. They live across here [points on a map]. I have to breach the ASBO if I want to go and see them.'

Another offender who was given an ASBO for prolific burglary and robberies claimed it was unfair to be at risk of imprisonment for behaviour that is not itself criminal. He had this to say:

'As far as I'm concerned, if I'm walking up the road and I'm not supposed to be on that road but I'm not breaking the law, why should they breach me? If I'm down the shop and I steal something ... breach me if I've done something wrong.'

In some instances, the interviewees felt that such conditions were an erosion of their human rights. This clearly angered some of the offenders. According to one 18-year-old male who had received an ASBO for persistent begging:

'On the actual ASBO the only thing that wasn't good was the curfew. I think that's breach of human rights, really, to be in at a certain time. I think that was the only thing I didn't really respond to.'

A similar view was expressed by a 28-year-old male who had received an ASBO for repeated burglaries and robberies:

'I just haven't got the time or the inclination to muck about down there trying to get permission off somebody that I don't think should have any fucking rights to stop me from going there anyway. I'm paying rent on the place but I'm not allowed to go there.'

Three offenders claimed the order to be so restrictive that a prison sentence would be preferable. As one 18-year-old offender, serving a custodial sentence for breaching the curfew condition of his ASBO, said:

'If you go to jail once, you don't care if you go again do you?... If I do breach it and I come back, then I want to do my ASBO time in prison because it is driving me up the wall, you don't understand, man. It is harder than being in prison, that's why I don't want to go back out there....'

Another male respondent aged 37, who had received a post-conviction ASBO for prolific begging, complained about the inactivity associated with an ASBO and stated that he would have preferred a sanction that involved attending group meetings. It was implied that this lack of activity had some impact on his propensity to continue begging:

'Personally, I think an ASBO is worse than probation. You have so much to occupy yourself with, if you are on a DTTO, you are in groups, give you support, to help you stay away from crime and I think that is quite therapeutic. Them sort of things are helpful but with an ASBO, there is no activity, no groups. I am just still begging. Rather than give you an ASBO, they could set up a unit and put the conditions around attending the unit.'

Some offenders considered ASBOs to be a weaker alternative than a criminal sanction and they were therefore not taken seriously by either offenders or their families. Thirteen per cent of interviewees responded to the order in this way, some referring to it as a joke. This attitude was more common among younger interviewees; however, older, more prolific or substance-misusing offenders also tended to hold this view. One 17-year-old male reported that:

'They [the family] just smiled and said, "You got an ASBO". They thought it was a joke.'

One male, aged 17, who was serving a custodial sentence for breach of his post-conviction ASBO, which he had received as a consequence of a series of driving offences and the theft of motor vehicles, stated:

> 'You think it's a joke and that but when you get the ASBO it is serious, because you know you are getting targeted.'

In contrast to these negative perceptions, 14% of respondent regarded receiving of the ASBO as being in some way beneficial. For some, it was seen as a fair response to their behaviour; for others, it was a relief, particularly when a custodial sentence was avoided. One 19-year-old male offender given a post-conviction ASBO for violent disorder states,

> 'I was a bit relieved because they wanted to put me in prison. It's hard, but I'd rather get an ASBO and that, and tagging than go to prison. But I was pissed off because I couldn't go in that area.'

At least two offenders reported the order to be a 'wake-up call', alerting them to the need to change their behaviour or face the consequences. A further 6% of responses indicated that the offender was concerned about the consequences of breaching the order. One female offender serving a custodial sentence for drug-related thefts and assault realised that she could be given up to five years in prison for a breach of her order and had this to say:

> 'This is the wake-up call because my mind is set because if I go out there and drink and take drugs, I am back to prison for up to five years. I ain't doing it. It is tough anyway being here and I have 15 months. I ain't coming back.'

The respondents who reported positive attitudes towards their ASBO were usually those who did not breach their orders, or whose breaching rapidly diminished. As one young male given a post-conviction ASBO for graffiti reported:

> 'I think it was fair. It was my way of paying back for the damage and not having to pay the fine. It was a kind of second chance.'

In this case, the issuing of a Referral Order together with a post-conviction ASBO appeared to encourage the offender to change both his attitude and his behaviour and realise the consequence of his actions.

> 'It has been really helpful. It has kept me away from the wrong crowd. I used to meet different people at specific places and do it with them. It was a proper little culture. Now I don't hang around with them any more…. It has changed completely my attitude and behaviour towards society. I wouldn't think about going out and doing things like that again. I have grown up a lot. I know when to say no and I know it is better to say no and walk away.'

Responses to the conditions of the order

Respondents were asked to identify the number of conditions that were specified in their order. As Figure 3.1 indicates, the modal number of conditions included in the orders examined was two, and the median three. No condition was imposed differentially according to gender or ethnicity. Interestingly, those on whom geographic restrictions were placed were significantly older than those not restricted in that way. This was the only condition showing a significant age difference.

Figure 3.1: Number of ASBOs conditions

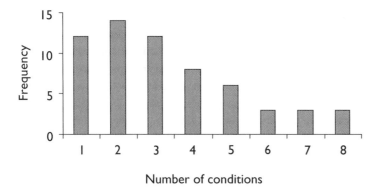

Figure 3.2 shows the distribution of conditions by type. The most common condition was not to visit a particular area. The condition not to engage in a type of crime was seen by a number of respondents as odd since it prohibited offenders from engaging in an activity that was already designated as a criminal offence and therefore already prohibited.

Figure 3.2: Distribution of conditions by type

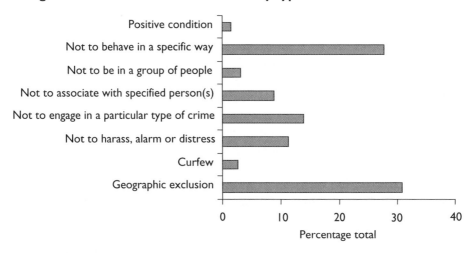

Approximately a quarter of those interviewed expressed some degree of dissatisfaction with the conditions they had been given. This was either as the result of their own concerns, through discussions with their legal representatives or as a result of a challenge to the conditions made by a magistrate. The interviews indicated that in 13 cases offenders had begun to involve their solicitors in negotiations (with differing results) as they felt that they had a right to enter a certain area or return home at a certain time. Other issues that were being contested were the boundaries of the areas of exclusion, either because they were seen as somewhat arbitrary, as no offences had been carried out in the areas of exclusion, or because they were simply unclear. One young male offender who had contacted his solicitor in order to appeal against conditions in his order reported:

> 'They told me I could contest it. They told my solicitor, the solicitor said he would take it back to court.... To tell you the truth I want to take it back to court and get [area] and [area] taken off. I don't care about the estates and hanging around with them people – that isn't bothering me [but] I can't even go to school because I will be breaching it, just being on a bus, that's me breaching it again.... The only problem is, that day I didn't turn up to contest the ASBO. I never knew where the court was ....'

One of the frequently contested aspects of an ASBO is the duration of the order, which is usually in the range of three to five years. However, offenders (and agency staff) reported cases where 10-year ASBOs were given, or ASBOs were given 'until further notice', which was interpreted by some as meaning for 'life'. When asked how long his ASBO was for, one offender responded:

> 'Forever. If they find me selling travel cards because it cause problems in the station, they will put me inside.'

Some offenders felt that they were unable to abide by the conditions specified in the ASBO for any length of time and that they had a good chance of ending up in prison. In the words of one interviewee:

> 'It looks like you have got another prison sentence because there's no way I can go through that ASBO without stopping within that map ... within five years ...'

These issues, which were raised by offenders, have also been raised by Lord Chief Justice Thomas, who recently produced guidance for Crown, magistrates and county courts to improve the way in which conditions are written (Thomas, 2005). It has been recognised by ASBO recipients and agency staff alike that many of the ASBO conditions have been poorly constructed, written and explained, and that this has a serious impact on their enforcement and on the perceptions of both offenders and communities. These findings support the views of agency staff expressed in Chapter 2.

Impact of ASBOs on offenders

It became evident in the course of the interviews that ASBOs had a differential impact on different offenders and that while in some cases they encouraged a change of behaviour, this was not always accompanied by a change of attitude. It was clear that the impact on offenders could not be reduced to mutually exclusive alternatives of success or failure. As with other sanctions, it was anticipated that not only were ASBOs unlikely to turn persistent and long-term offenders into non-offenders but that it was necessary to examine the various dimensions of change. For this reason, we developed a fivefold typology by which to assess the differential impact of ASBOs.

As Table 3.3 shows, there is an indication from our sample of a self-reported improvement in specific forms of offending behaviour and attitudes towards offending among those offenders who have received ASBOs. However, there is a simultaneous deterioration in the group as a whole in their psychological state and social circumstances. In many of the interviews, offenders reported improvements in one or more aspects of their behaviour, while at the same time reporting deterioration in other areas. It was unusual for an offender to report an across-the-board improvement in all five of the categories shown in Table 3.3.

Table 3.3: Self-reported change

	Offending	Substance abuse	Psychological	Attitudes towards ASB	Social circum- stances
Reduced/ improved	26	15	14	28	2
No change	20	26	22	22	5
Increased/ worsened	7	4	28	14	13
Total responses	53	45	64	64	20

Out of the total of 66 offenders, 25 had decreased their involvement in the 'trigger' offence for which the ASBO was issued, 12 had reduced their general level of offending and 28 reported a positive change in attitude. While these responses suggest a more positive attitude to receiving an ASBO than might be expected, three important qualifications should be attached to these findings. The first is that an improvement often involved a reduction in the frequency or the seriousness of offences individuals were engaged in. Only in a limited number of cases did respondents report stopping offending altogether. Ideally, in future studies based on a larger random sample, it would be necessary to construct a scale of improvement that could begin to measure the degree of change for different offenders.

The second qualification is that a number of these offenders were given ASBOs at the peak of their offending and that over time there would have been a propensity for offending to reduce without any formal intervention or for the level of offending to be reduced by deploying an alternative sanction. In some cases, the nature of offending probably could not have got much worse and therefore almost any formal intervention would have probably accompanied a positive response in these cases.

The third qualification is that nine of the respondents were in prison when interviewed and for this reason were no longer committing the offences for which they had received the ASBO. It is also the case that although some expressed a change of attitude, we know from previous research that people's attitudes may change while they are in prison and revert back on release. We should, therefore, treat the responses of these nine respondents with some caution.

We examined these responses in order to identify if there were specific offences in relation to which the ASBO might be most effective. No identifiable pattern emerged with the exception of ticket touting, where five respondents said that they had stopped engaging in this activity as a result of receiving an ASBO. (This high number of ticket touts was a function of including in the sample a significant number of British Transport Police cases.)

In the case study below, the respondent reports a positive change in both behaviour and attitude. However, he also reports that the ASBO has had a negative impact on his psychological state and social circumstances, by restricting his movement and not offering him adequate support.

Youth disorder: a case study

The subject is a 16-year-old male who received an ASBO for disorderly conduct towards residents and shopkeepers, and damage to shops, houses and buses. He was unemployed and lived with his mother in a council-owned property on a large estate.

His initial reaction to the order was that it was unfair, as he did not consider himself to have committed the offence. However, when he realised the possible implications for his family as council tenants, he decided to keep himself 'squeaky clean'.

The subject reported that the police were watching his house and as a result he stayed at home, often in bed until 1pm. He had no money and was not actively seeking work. He felt isolated and restricted in his activities because of the ASBO. He reported that he had not been offered any support or guidance or any formal visits from the police or social workers since he had been given the order.

From the responses provided by interviewees, it was possible to identify three broad groups: those whose anti-social behaviour increased, those whose had decreased and those who reported no change at all in their behaviour. Our aim was to try to identify the circumstances in which these changes took place and to link these changes to more general changes in attitude.

Increased anti-social behaviour

Seven of those interviewed reported that their offending behaviour had increased after being issued with an ASBO. This group often reported intentionally behaving in contravention of their order. As one 37-year-old male who had been given an ASBO for persistent begging stated:

> 'I want to do certain things, just to be arrested because of this stupid ASBO. It is like a little child, you can't do this, you can't do that, don't touch this, don't touch that. That is what it's like.'

Young people and their families in particular reported feeling stigmatised as a result of receiving an ASBO. Some were inclined to live up to the label they had been given. One mother reported: ↘ labelling theory

> 'When they [her two sons] are branded with an ASBO it gives them thoughts like, "Well, I am an anti-social behaviour person, so I might as well go and re-offend. I've got this label, the police won't leave me alone, I might as well go carry up to the label they have branded me with."'

Some offenders reported problems in understanding their order and what might be anti-social. They also reported feeling as if the ASBO had lowered the threshold for behaviour that could be considered serious, meaning that while they had stopped behaving in the manner associated with the ASBO they were still getting in trouble, often with more serious consequences for lesser offences. One offender, who was given a post-conviction ASBO as well as a Detention and Training Order for a series of robberies and burglaries, said:

> 'If I am getting locked up for these little things, I might as well just go and do a big thing worth something than keep going for some stupid petty shit.'

Decreased anti-social behaviour

In our sample there was no particular age group that conspicuously reduced their level of offending. For 'trigger' offences, there was a relatively even reduction across age groups. In relation to other forms of offending, the 16-20 age group and the 31-35 age group showed the most significant decrease. However, in relation to attitudes, the 16-20 age group showed a marked change, with 65% reporting a positive change of attitude, as Table 3.4 indicates. Only a few of those in this age group reported drug problems, although five did report using cannabis and one had used ecstasy and hallucinogenic drugs but reported that his substance use had decreased following the imposition of the ASBO.

Table 3.4 Offences and attitude since ASBO, by age group

	Trigger offences since ASBO	Other offences since ASBO	Improved attitude	Total number in age group
10 to 15	5	1	4	10
16 to 20	4	3	15	23
21 to 25	3	0	2	6
26 to 30	5	1	3	7
31 to 35	4	4	1	7
36 to 40	4	2	1	7
Over 40	1	1	2	6
Total	26	12	28	66

Many of the young people who were given ASBOs had been 'hanging around' in groups and claimed that they had nowhere else to go. This frequently led to neighbourhood complaints about their behaviour. In the words of one 16-year-old:

> 'You see that area down there, everyone used to hang down there, well people still do but there is too many people there but they moan about us sitting there which means people can't sit down there, so we move to stairwells and they still moan. Anywhere we go, people moan. There is nothing for us to do on this estate, it's pony.'

This reaction resulted in him moving elsewhere with the group until he was eventually given an ASBO. While the offender's initial reaction to the order was that it was disproportionate and unfair, particularly as he was the only one given an order, he has been deterred from continuing his anti-social behaviour because of the threat of prison. In his words:

> 'It is just that I am paranoid, I don't really want to go to prison. Never been and don't want to go there. So I keep my head down until my ASBO is finished but probably by the time it is I'll be too old to be hanging around the street. I'll have a job and that.'

What seems to have worked for this group is the combination of deterrence (prison, loss of freedom, potential loss of housing), the severity of the sanction itself, and the degree of support in changing behaviour and learning about the consequences of their actions on individuals and communities. Most of the young offenders in this group reported that they had simply 'grown out of it' and suggested that the changes that had taken place were largely the result of normal processes of maturation. In a few cases, the ASBO had provided a 'wake-up call' or acted as a catalyst to speed up these changes.

Among this group of offenders, many had received support services of some kind in conjunction with their order. This was usually a Supervision Order or a Referral Order, ensuring regular contact with a worker from the Youth Offending Team, which may have helped the young people to develop skills or a better understanding of their order and the consequences of their actions. The imposition of the ASBO, particularly in conjunction with another order or appropriate parental support, appears to encourage personal accountability and a positive change in behaviour and attitude. One 17-year-old who felt the ASBO had helped him stay out of trouble described the experience of getting his ASBO:

> 'We were getting arrested every day. Until one day they took us all to court, and we were all in the same room. And we all got an ASBO, we all had to go to Crown Court for it, even though we was youths. The communities put it on us, stop you getting into trouble around the community, because it brings trouble to them, nicking cars and all that.'

He also describes the regret he feels for his behaviour and the impact it had on his family:

> 'They [the local police] call my mum by her first name. If I could go back to last year I wouldn't have done what I have done ... an ASBO I think it knuckles you down. In a way I'm glad I have got it.... It has stopped me from getting into trouble. If I weren't on one I would probably still be driving around.... I think you grow out of it, if I could go back I would. I'd tell kids aged 13 not to do it....'

Towards the end of the interview, after discussing his work with the Youth Offending Team, the other sanctions he had received and the behaviour that had led up to him getting an order, the offender acknowledged his responsibility for his behaviour and described the ASBO as a fair and reasonable sanction.

> 'Yeah, it was fair because you only do it to yourself. You only get the ASBO because of what you have done, not because of anyone else. It is an easy way to keep you out of trouble and keep you out of jail....'

There were cases where those served with ASBOs reported that the order had encouraged them to change their behaviour through the setting of boundaries. A male, aged 16, who was given a post-conviction ASBO for graffiti stated:

> 'They put a restriction on me that if I was caught carrying pens and things then I'd be back in court. I didn't think that would be acceptable so I really had to buckle up and make sure it didn't happen again....'

Another male, aged 17, given a post-conviction ASBO for nuisance behaviour connected to a violent assault, reported that:

'A couple of my friends are on ASBOs, and it has calmed them down because they know if they breach they are going inside. For someone my age, it ain't a pretty thought. If you get an ASBO it is because you have done a lot wrong.'

In the more successful cases, where the specific behaviour ceased, the ASBO tended to be associated with a package of interventions that dealt with the underlying causes of the anti-social behaviour and helped the offender change. In one case, the offender was issued with a post-conviction ASBO by the court for damaging trains and railway sidings with graffiti. The ASBO was issued as an alternative to a large fine that the family could not afford to pay. The courts also imposed a Referral Order as a result of which the offender was required to undertake reparation activities and work with a member of the Youth Offending Team on interventions to prevent reoffending. The offender reported the following effects of the Referral Order:

'I have grown up a lot. I know when to say "no" and I know it is better to say "no" and walk away. I learnt assertiveness on the Referral Order, and how to deal with peer pressure.'

The offender also reported that the biggest factor responsible for his change in behaviour was the impact the ASBO had had on his mother, who was well respected in her local community, following the reporting of his details in the local newspaper. He reported that going to court made him realise the costs of the damage he had caused, the ASBO gave him clear boundaries for his behaviour and the Referral Order helped him say no to the pressures of his peers, who continued to encourage him to do graffiti. In this case, however, it appears important that the offender had a close and respectful relationship with his family and community.

A factor that was seen by many offenders as contributing to their decreased anti-social behaviour was the strength of the partnership approach. The case study below provides an example of how a coordinated approach can be effective in changing behaviour.

Youth substance misuse: a case study

The situation: At the age of 15, the young person received a two-year ASBO for persistent begging, burglary and harassment. He first came to the attention of the police at age 13. He admitted heavy use of crack during the period of his anti-social behaviour and reports first using cannabis at age 11. He was also from a family with multiple and complex social problems. His mother was dependent on alcohol, used cannabis and crack, was offending and had a long-term illness. Some of his siblings had been taken into local authority care and the remaining family had been evicted from local authority housing for anti-social behaviour. As a result, they lost contact with support services in the borough.

The intervention: Prior to the ASBO, the subject was given a Supervision Order and housed away from the area in a project designed to provide education and housing. Initially, the ASBO was requested by a local police officer based on evidence provided by a victim whom the subject had assaulted. The ASBO was intended as a way of controlling his anti-social behaviour, which had continued despite the other interventions.

When the interim ASBO was served, the Youth Offending Team opposed the application and sought adjournment of the case. The local ASBU identified the subject to be vulnerable and produced a consultation document inviting other stakeholders to attend and share information about the case. This raised huge issues in relation to partnership working and opened up a philosophical fault line between enforcement-based and client-based services. The ASBU worked to resolve these issues and specific conditions were written into the ASBO to support other interventions that had been put in place. The offender was placed in a children's home away from the borough where he was offending. He was helped to enrol in college and was provided with regular contact with a youth project. The anti-social behaviour team wrote a curfew condition into the ASBO to support the workers in the children's home in managing his behaviour.

The impact: The subject reported that while he was relieved to be given an ASBO, he frequently breached it by staying out past the curfew and approaching people to beg. He often returned to his area to visit his mother and to continue begging and taking drugs. He reported being caught by his key worker smoking cannabis (both a breach of the ASBO conditions and a criminal offence), but was not reported for doing so. He also reported being stopped three or four times a day to be searched by the police. He acknowledged that he would be subject to further sanctions if he continued offending but that his drug habit was his priority. He reported that it was his mother's imprisonment that led to his change of behaviour. He recognised that he had been given his last chance by being given an ASBO and that the other sanctions had not worked. He believes that the ASBO came about because the agencies that were involved with him knew that prison would not be a suitable place for him and worked together to find an alternative. He admits the ASBO made him realise that his behaviour was not appropriate and put a boundary in place for him.

The subject is now living independently, attending college full time and working part time. He no longer uses drugs or commits any form of anti-social behaviour or crime. He still has regular contact with the services that helped him through his experience.

This case highlights the complex issues that may be associated with engaging in anti-social behaviour and offending. The ASBU responsible for this case identified and overcame many barriers to effective partnership working, adopted a multi-agency approach and created a balanced outcome that benefited both the offender and the community.

Some respondents pointed out that the threat of an order was sometimes enough to persuade people to change their behaviour. As was pointed out by a few respondents, once offenders are placed on the ASBO register, the relationship between offender and community changes and that in itself can act as effective 'wake-up call' to offenders without the need to pursue cases through to completion.

No change in anti-social behaviour

Nearly a third of those interviewed indicated that there had been no change in their propensity to offend or commit anti-social behaviour. Many of those interviewed had substance misuse problems and reported that the ASBO was ineffective in changing their anti-social or offending behaviour, as it did not tackle the underlying cause of their behaviour. In the words of one interviewee, an adult male given a CRASBO for begging and who admits using both crack and heroin:

> 'I don't think the ASBO has affected me, I suppose it has in a sense because I could do without being arrested but apart from that, I don't really care. I do care if I get arrested but I don't care about the ASBO because I need to do what I need to do and I need what I need. What they say and what they do ain't going to get me off the brown or the white.'

Among those who reported that their behaviour and pattern of offending had not changed and who did not have substance misuse issues were some offenders who had been diagnosed with psychological or interpersonal problems and those who claimed to have breached their orders regularly but avoided detection.

Geographic and functional displacement

Anti-social behaviour may be displaced either by crime type or location, or both. As noted above, some form of exclusion was the most frequent condition included in the orders in this sample. In all, 54 of 66 (82%) of orders contained some element of geographical exclusion. It was also evident in the interviews with offenders that a number of them had changed the nature of their offending as a result of receiving an ASBO. However, it is difficult to gauge the exact extent of functional displacement, since many of those interviewed had substantial histories of offending and had engaged in a number of different forms of offending before they received their ASBOs.

Most of those whose orders contained some form of exclusion found themselves excluded from an area where they had lived for most, if not all, of their life. Consequently, they found the impact of geographical exclusion quite difficult to manage. As one male offender aged 21 who was sent to prison for making bomb threats put it:

> 'When I got the first ASBO, I was banned from the whole area and they take your flat away, everything. You have to start again, I was homeless. After that, I moved to [an inner-city borough] and started pissing people off there.'

This offender had been issued with an ASBO banning him from an entire rural county. Consequently, he moved to an inner-city borough where he had been served another ASBO for his behaviour. By moving from the area where they are known to enforcement or other agency staff, offenders may also leave behind the support services that can help them reduce their anti-social behaviour. In one interview, an offender who had received an ASBO for ticket touting and drug misuse made the following comment:

> 'Now I can't tout. I can't do the checkouts, can't beg. I can't grasp it. It is causing me so much hassle because I am having to adjust my criminality towards my circumstances. I have to make my money. I shouldn't have got an ASBO, not me, a drug user? Because I am going to find it most difficult of all people.... I shouldn't have been banned from the area. I should have been given a support network ... an ASBO is just moving me to another area.'

In some cases, offenders reported that moving away from a particular community in which there had been a deterioration in relationships with neighbours, or where there was a different social mix and different levels of tolerance, meant that their behaviour no longer caused harassment, alarm or distress to others.

One consequence of moving out of the area where the offender was known was that offenders were able to operate with relative anonymity. Several offenders reported knowing they would not be caught or could avoid detection.

There were also several cases in which offenders changed the form of their offending as a result of receiving an ASBO. In some cases, this involved offenders engaging in more serious offences, while in other cases, they desisted from relatively serious and persistent forms of offending and became involved in more minor and relatively infrequent forms of offending. For example, one offender who had changed from ticket touting to shoplifting and consequently became involved in a more high-risk but more lucrative activity explained that:

> 'You make the money quickly with the shoplifting. With the tickets, it is an hour, maybe two hours before you've got enough for a score, so you use more because

you earn more. Double the money because it only takes five minutes but you take the risk.'

Another adult male ticket tout reports:

'I take risks now. Stupid things like robbing people and I do not think of the consequences but maybe I get more for putting a knife in someone's neck … now I have done a lot to people … pick-pocketing people, robbing people, things I didn't do. When I can and the police aren't around I will do tickets, sometimes working for the dealer as the runner….'

As the case below indicates, some offenders are able to change their appearance or give false details in order to avoid detection.

Avoiding detection: a case study

The 15-year-old subject was issued a CRASBO on conviction for burglary. She has a history of offending including being arrested for robberies, ABH, GBH, criminal damage, drunk and disorderly and aggravated burglary.

Initially, she was relieved to have been spared a custodial sentence and felt anxious about having been put on a curfew. However, after realising that the police would not come to her house to check her whereabouts after 10pm, she frequently breached her order and continued to behave as she had in the past.

When she was recognised and stopped by the police she gave false details. She also admitted changing her appearance as a way of escaping detection.

In cases where the offender continued their anti-social behaviour, they might do so in the same manner or else make slight adjustments to their appearance. As one respondent who claimed to breach their order systematically explained:

'If I've got shoes and the trousers and that. It's a doddle to walk around the city. I've been up there a few times… Yeah, you look like you've just come out of your office sort of thing.'

Number and type of breaches

Official data on breaches obviously only include cases that have come to the attention of the authorities and have been formally prosecuted with evidence beyond reasonable doubt. The actual rate of breach must be a great deal higher, and indeed the interviews with those who had received an ASBO support this suggestion. There was a significant difference between the numbers of prosecuted breaches and self-disclosed breaches. The number of official breaches is largely a reflection of the level of enforcement or the quality of the conditions written into an order, rather than the behaviour of the offender. One young woman, whose ASBO included an area of exclusion and a curfew order, explained:

> 'They arrest you, you're in a cell for hours until the court hearing. The prosecution then says his bit, then my defence says their bit then the three magistrates say ok, bail. They just keep giving me bail. I must have breached it loads of times, I have not been convicted for breach of ASBO.'

Some 61% of the sample acknowledged one or more breaches of conditions, and 52% had attracted 'official' breach action, with 11 people claiming three or more such breaches.[2] Because the dates of the orders' imposition were not available, it was not possible to look more precisely at the relationship between breach action and order, corrected for length of the relevant risk period.

Those on orders were asked whether they had been offered support services while on the order. Those who were offered such services tended to be less likely to 'officially' breach their orders than those who were not. An almost identical pattern emerged with self-reported breaches.

In relation to breaches, offenders can be divided into three fairly discrete groups: those who deliberately and consciously breach; those determined not to breach; and those who breach unintentionally.

Intentional breach

A large proportion of the offenders interviewed (61%) reported regularly breaching their order. This occurred for a number of different reasons. For some, it was a reaction to their order – for example, feeling wronged or unjustly labelled, or being subjected to unreasonable conditions. One young man, aged 15, given an ASBO in conjunction with a Detention and Training Order (DTTO) for robberies and thefts, expressed his propensity to breach in the following terms:

> "Say for example that one of the shops on one side are closed and the other shops are open on the other side. What am I supposed to do? Get a travel card and go to

---

[2] As has already been reported, the sample used in this study is slightly skewed as a result of interviews undertaken with offenders in prison, some of whom had received a custodial sentence for breaching their ASBO. In application, this means that the self-reported and 'official' breach figures are probably closer in this sample than they would be in the overall population. However, further research would be required to determine whether this is actually the case.

another area to buy milk and bread? I would just rather cross the road and buy it, but they make it just hassle.'

Similarly, an adult ticket tout made this comment:

'I have to go within that 500 yards of the tube station that I have been banned from. It won't actually have stopped me…. There is a shop there, my favourite chicken shop. I am still going to go there.'

Substance misusers more frequently admitted breaching their ASBOs than any other group of offenders, with nearly three quarters (74%) admitting breaching their order. The offender interviews indicated that this group is likely to breach the conditions of their order either to visit drug markets, or to earn money legitimately or through acquisitive crime, or as a result of being unclear about their order conditions because of the effects of drugs or alcohol. Some of these offenders breached conditions so that they could access services within the area of exclusion, or in order to visit family or friends. For a significant proportion of this group, the threat of prison no longer acted as a deterrent. As one 28-year-old polydrug user stated:

'I'm breaking it every week but I will keep on doing that until it finishes. I don't want to get caught but if needs arise where I can't wait…. I don't want a life of misery not going to be able to go where I want to go.'

In the words of another heroin user:

'Every day I would go in, get what I need and go home. Don't go back. One stop there and make sure I had what I needed for the day, you know, I have what I have got, to do what I do…. I would go into offices for 30 seconds and bang, bang, bang, your laptop is gone and I've got it and I am going home. It would be a few grand a day.'

In a few cases, interviewees reported that their offending behaviour was an endemic part of their everyday life. For example, one interviewee admitted committing robberies to 'top up' his living standards. To do this, he regularly entered a shopping district within his area of exclusion to commit robberies and purchase fashionable clothes.

Determined not to breach

Approximately a quarter of those in the sample expressed a strong commitment not to breach the conditions of their order. The two recurring factors influencing this decision were the nature of the conditions included in the order and the availability of good support networks of family and friends. In a number of cases where individuals had good support networks, they also reported that they would not breach because of family responsibilities, or because they wanted to keep their job or their place in college. In a few cases, offenders stated that they were determined not to breach their order because they wanted to avoid a more serious sanction, such as imprisonment, or because they were aiming to have the order revoked in order to return to the area from which they had been excluded by the ASBO.

In one case that typified the determination of some offenders not to breach, a 16-year-old male living with his parents was given a two-year ASBO on conviction for criminal damage and graffiti to trains. He stated:

> 'I have nothing to do with graffiti. I have moved on from that now because it [the ASBO] had such a huge impact on my family…. I look back on how childish it was. Mum went through a really tough phase, the court went on for eight months and mum wondered what she had done wrong for me to be behaving like that…. The ASBO has put me straight…. The look on her [mum] in court did me in. She did nothing to deserve it.'

Another strong incentive not to breach was the threat of a parent or family losing their home. Several of those interviewed reported this as being a strong deterrent to their continuing anti-social behaviour. An 18-year-old male given an ASBO for being involved with a large group of youths causing nuisance on their housing estate said:

> 'I can't go out and meet my mates and they can't come here. It has made me think twice about getting into trouble. My mum will be in trouble with the council if I breach…. I don't want the family to be moved.'

Unintentional breach

From the sample, only a small number of breaches could be claimed to be 'unintentional'. Such unintentional breaches were mainly the result of a lack of understanding of the order, its conditions, or of the consequences of a breach. Some offenders appeared confused. One 15-year-old, for example, who had been diagnosed as suffering from a form of conduct disorder, asked the interviewer during the course of the interview the meaning of 'harass, alarm or distress'. In his words:

> 'I'm breaching it. That's how I'm getting into more trouble. So I am not going a good way, trying not to breach it, I am breaching it…. I didn't really notice not so long ago, until I got breached for it. That was the only way I could understand it.'

Unintentional breaches were also reported by some of those involved in alcohol or drug abuse. A worker at a wet centre suggested that those with chronic alcohol issues may also have difficulty understanding their order and made the following comment:

'They placed the behavioural ASBO on him and it's been difficult ever since to be able to do much work with him. He didn't understand the ASBO ... we think he's probably got "wet-brain" syndrome [alcoholic dementia] and just didn't understand that he's not allowed to drink out there. He thought the place that he wasn't allowed to drink was on the Apollo and on the station and he couldn't understand it's the whole of [London borough] that he's not allowed to drink in. He didn't understand it, so of course he consistently got caught.'

Impact on personal, social and family life

The impact on the personal, social, economic and family life of those served with ASBOs is important to consider because these factors may contribute to the person's propensity to reoffend or engage in anti-social behaviour in the future. The offenders interviewed reported a wide range of both positive and negative impacts on their personal and social lives, including changes in family relationships. In some cases, it was reported that the ASBO had made a positive impact on family life. This was particularly the case in families where there was already a level of trust and support. One young offender reported that:

'I am going out more with my friends and I have been going out with my family. It has brought us all closer together and there is an element of trust there in my family. It has had a big impact.'

In another case in which an offender was repeatedly arrested for breaching the conditions of his ASBO, the family became increasingly upset:

'My family, because I keep getting nicked for breach of ASBO, they are upset and think I am getting into trouble ... just because I go to this place when I forgot I shouldn't be there, it is a crime.'

As a mother whose two sons had both received ASBOs put it:

'It didn't just put an ASBO on them, it put an ASBO on all of us.'

One recurring theme that emerged from the interviews with offenders was increased police attention. One 18-year-old offender who had been given an ASBO for prolific begging reported the consequences of this:

'I was going home one day and I think my curfew was 10 o'clock and I got home at two minutes past 10 and the police were waiting at my front door so I had to get held in custody overnight.'

Another suggested that even despite improving his behaviour he had become an increased target to the police as a result of his order.

> 'I get stopped every day when I am not even in the area, maybe up to twice a day. I don't get it. I have kept myself out of trouble.'

Other respondents reported increased victimisation after receiving an ASBO. One 18-year-old male reported the extreme consequence of being stabbed, which, he claimed, was the result of being targeted by the community because of his ASBO.

> 'I have had so many fights over things I have never even done, I have been stabbed since the ASBO. People are blaming me for nicking their mopeds.'

Another, aged 13, who had been excluded from the area where he had grown up and with which he was familiar, felt that the exclusion from this area made him more vulnerable to becoming a victim of crime.

> 'When I first got my ASBO I got a new bike and 'cos I weren't allowed to ride it on the roads, I had to go back roads, through alleys and stuff and when I walked through an alley I got robbed for my bike.'

Some offenders reported increased depression, paranoia and stress, while others reported tensions in their relationships and within their families. This was particularly severe when there had been media publicity or the distribution of fliers by the local authority.

> 'I think about it all the time. That's why I take my tablets all the time. I take more because I'm more depressed. They're nerve tablets.'

One ASBO, which has been referred to above, centred on street drinking and was seen by the various agencies involved as a success. As a result of the initiative, it was claimed that not only were the street drinkers dispersed by the intervention but also that some of those given ASBOs improved their behaviour. One particular woman who had a history of heavy drinking, violence, obscenity and urinating in public had reportedly changed her behaviour as a result of receiving the ASBO. By chance, she had moved to a neighbouring borough and was one of the people we interviewed. She said in her interview that her behaviour had been moderated, that she was drinking less, and living in a hostel rather than on the streets. She was receiving some help for her mental health problems and had renewed her relationship with her 19-year-old daughter. However, in her interview she stated:

> 'I have been arrested twice for breach of the ASBO and the case has been thrown out twice. Thrown out. I went to jail on remand for five weeks and lost me accommodation. So there is me, back on the street. I walked out of the court with nothing. No

discharge grant. No accommodation. No nothing. Five weeks remand in jail. A few weeks ago they did it again. They nicked me and it was an unlawful arrest.'

Apparently, she was arrested for breaching her ASBO in an area outside of the exclusion zone stipulated in her order. She claims that since receiving the ASBO she has kept out of the exclusion zone and refrained from engaging in violence. She added:

'I have behaved myself. In fact in another eight months' time, if I keep my nose clean, not get arrested, not go to jail, I can appeal against the five years.'

She agreed that the ASBO had had a positive impact in her case and that she had complied with the conditions in order to get the ASBO revoked, so that she could return to the borough in which the order was issued to be with her old friends. At the age of 40 she had decided that she did not want to go to prison any more.

Many of those interviewed were keen to put the ASBO behind them by getting back into work, education or training, or by moving away from the area where they had lived during the period of the ASBO in order to make a 'fresh start'. However, interviewees reported several potential barriers to this, including discrimination by employers, exclusion from jobs, restrictions on travel as a result of geographic conditions, and housing problems.

One female interviewee who had been imprisoned for breach of ASBO felt that the area of exclusion specified in her order would make it more difficult to find work on her release from prison.

'A lot has happened since I have been in here and I just want to get out, get a job and go home and go back to college and be normal again. The ASBO – sometimes they can help you - in a way they can – but also if they are going to ban me from the city, then I can't get to appointments or get a job. It is where all the offices and shops are. It is going to move me backwards.'

Similarly, one interviewee aged 37 felt that the positive impacts of the ASBO had been countered by the problems he faced in finding employment. For him, this was directly the result of a condition that prevented him entering the area where work was available.

'It has helped me but in the long term it's stopped me from getting a job and everything so it's swings and roundabouts.... I had a job open to me but it was West London and surrounding areas ... and I'm like, "I can't, I'm on an ASBO"'.

Some interviewees reported problems with housing after being given an ASBO, blaming the ASBO for their not being able to obtain local authority or housing association accommodation. One interviewee who was issued with a post-conviction

ASBO for commercial burglary reported the following experience when attempting to move from London to Manchester:

> 'Well, when I went back to Manchester as a result of the ASBO to try and settle down, I applied for a flat. I viewed it and decided to take it. Half an hour later they said, "You can't have one because you have an ASBO in London…" They were going to give me a flat, the council. Went to view it, nice and centrally located and I said I will take it but they phoned me at 2.30 and said, "Sorry Mr [Name], we can't give you the flat, you have an ASBO in London"'.

Making an application for housing to a local authority or housing association requires that a tenant does not behave anti-socially, cause a nuisance or harass other people. Part of the process of application requires the tenant to provide references, in this case, the local authority where he was housed in London, which presumably informed Manchester about the subject's ASBO despite it being unrelated to his behaviour as a tenant. For some, such barriers to employment, training, housing and support may propel them back into offending despite their desire to make a legitimate income and settle down.

It was evident that the exclusionary elements associated with ASBOs could in some cases compound the marginalised status of offenders and that this militated against their resettlement and reintegration. In those cases in which offenders expressed a genuine desire to reduce their offending and/or restructure their lives, they often found that the impact of the ASBO on their personal and social existence made it extremely difficult.

The impact on communities and victims

4

In order to find out how different community groups and victims felt about the effectiveness of Anti-Social Behaviour Orders (ASBOs), seven focus groups were conducted in communities that had been affected by high levels of anti-social behaviour and where ASBOs had been used. One of the focus groups was not directly related to specific ASBO cases, but was included in the survey to provide some insight into the attitudes of residents towards ASBOs in locations not directly affected by anti-social behaviour. Fourteen in-depth interviews with victims and complainants were also carried out. Each victim interview directly corresponds to one or more of the 38 ASBO cases.

Community consultation and reporting

As noted above, most of the partnerships made an effort to elicit the views of local residents and to engage them in addressing anti-social behaviour. The level of consultation varied considerably among the boroughs surveyed, with some establishing local community forums across the borough, while in other boroughs the level of involvement was very limited. It was also the case, as we have seen, that practitioners were in a number of cases generally dismissive of the apparently trivial and minor incidents they wanted controlled. Generally, local residents were seen by practitioners as being relatively intolerant, with a tendency to focus on relatively 'trivial' incidents

One strategy that some councils and Borough Command Units (BCUs) have introduced is dedicated telephone lines for people to report incidents of anti-social behaviour. The introduction of these telephone lines is often accompanied by a leafleting of residents to inform them of their existence and to encourage their use. However, there was found to be a discrepancy between the perception of the role of these dedicated telephone lines between practitioners and the public. Whereas the public appear to believe that when they report an incident it will generate a response and that something will be done about it, for the council the reports on these lines are used mainly as an intelligence-gathering exercise and as a way of monitoring incidents. There is normally no intention of providing an identifiable response to any report or even a series of reports. Residents find these so-called 'hot lines' frustrating and ineffective. As one resident put it:

> 'It's not a hot line it's a cold line. I mean they register it but when you see something that's virtually a crime happening on the street you want the police to come and sort it out quickly before anyone is damaged or hurt.'

Just as most residents want a rapid response in relation to the incidents they report, so many want ASBOs used quickly and effectively to deal with their concerns. Practitioners repeatedly emphasised that they thought that members of the public had unrealistic expectations of what ASBOs might achieve and how quickly they could be issued. Despite the fact that we conducted the focus groups in areas where a significant number of ASBOs had been issued, residents still tended to feel that not enough was being done and that ASBOs, by and large, had only brought temporary and limited relief from anti-social behaviour.

Interviewees from agencies made only passing reference to 'naming and shaming' offenders and the implication appears to be that most are not in favour of this sanction. However, the residents interviewed were generally more in favour of 'naming and shaming' measures, partly because they felt it was an effective sanction in itself and partly because it assisted in the identification of persistent offenders as well as playing a part in the enforcement of breaches. As a member of one focus group who had attended several Take a Stand conferences stated:

> 'What I think they need to do as well is to "name and shame" because I've been to quite a lot of Take a Stand conferences and there are places like Plymouth, Bristol and other parts of the country that do "name and shame". Our borough seems not to take that policy and yet the police sector meetings and at other meetings residents and people in the community are saying they want it. Because if a person has got an ASBO people need to know that this person has an ASBO because they have offended so many times. They have caused grievance to people's lives so as I said the boys on here go from estate to estate so if they go to a neighbouring estate how do they know what the person has done.... Our community don't know what their breaches are and it just upsets people.'

In most of the focus groups, the discussion gravitated towards the perceived problem of young people 'hanging around' estates. Residents reported a range of undesirable activities, which they associated with young people ranging from setting fire to cars, stealing cars, fighting and drinking. The issue that came up repeatedly was young people sitting in stairwells making a noise and drinking late at night and in some cases through the night. Residents said that they often did not know these young people and felt that many came from other estates. As they did not know them, they were fearful, particularly elderly residents and those living alone. The residents interviewed believed that the young people in the stairwells at night were probably taking drugs and therefore might act unpredictably if confronted.

It may be a function of the fact that most of the focus groups were conducted on council estates, but it was apparent that there was virtually no mention in these groups of activities such as begging or being drunk and disorderly. Indeed, there appeared to be a significant difference in the way in which activities in and around the council estate were viewed and those occurring on the street and other public spaces. It was evident that many of these residents felt vulnerable and trapped, even inside their own homes. It was also the case that some of the residents living on council estates felt that they were expected to put up with forms of bad behaviour that would not be tolerated in better-off areas. As one resident stated during one focus group session:

> 'I think that there is a perception that if you live on an estate, your threshold of trouble is supposed to be higher. We are supposed to put up with it more.'

Residents' groups were, by and large, critical of the police, magistrates and other practitioners who they felt lived outside the area and did not understand local problems. In relation to street prostitution, for example, one residents' group was very critical of the Greater London Assembly Report, which rejected the use of ASBOs for street prostitutes (London Assembly, 2005). The residents, who lived in a 'red-light' district, thought that the report was:

> 'Quite frankly disgraceful that the London Assembly sits there pontificating about what they believe is good for the electorate. And they don't even live in the areas affected by street prostitution.'

Community expectations and changing levels of tolerance

Respondents from all groups were critical of the rhetoric that surrounded ASBOs and the way they had been presented as a panacea. This was seen to raise community expectations. As one agency worker put it:

> 'I think people feel that they are going to actually do more than they actually do, that the ASBO is going to stop the behaviour then and there, end of story and perhaps the process is quicker and it's simpler than it actually is.'

Some respondents felt that anti-social behaviour campaigns that had been conducted locally as well as nationally on television, particularly those focusing on 'rowdy youths', had created the impression that all young people congregating in groups are problematic. This has resulted in a decrease in public tolerance towards young people. The general tendency to encourage people to report anti-social behaviour has also, no doubt, served to change sensibilities and reporting levels. Thus, when local authorities actively encourage residents to report anti-social behaviour incidents, they need to be aware that they may be helping to exacerbate a problem by increasing expectations in a way that they may be unable to manage.

The question of unrealistic expectations was raised by a number of respondents who felt that ASBOs were being widely presented as a 'quick fix' to a range of social issues and that they were relatively easy to procure. As one anti-social behaviour coordinator pointed out:

> 'It's a question of realistic expectations, isn't it, of what can be done? ... and the government's message on it is it gives to my view a very unrealistic impression of what can be done and how easy it is and "Bob's your Uncle, off you go to court ... two pieces of paper saying that this is what little Johnny did today and we get an ASBO and, my God, if he breaches it you're going inside!" ... it's not like that is it?'

It was suggested by some respondents that the publicity surrounding ASBOs had encouraged people to report potentially trivial incidents and expect that an ASBO might be forthcoming. There were also problems with monitoring and enforcing ASBOs and with making sure that they are appropriate rather than just trying to get more and more of them. The key, according to one community safety manager, is communication and keeping residents informed of developments in a clear and honest way, rather than pretending that the problem will still be solved overnight.

Problems with evidence, intimidation and enforcement

On one estate in London, four ASBOs had been issued, but members of the residents' group had several concerns, including the time taken to serve an ASBO, the problems of enforcement and the possibility of intimidation and reprisals. They stated that:

> 'ASBOs take too long to acquire because the two ASBOs that got done first on the estate was 18 months of recording what they were doing, what they wasn't doing and going back to city solicitors saying, "No, sorry, there's not enough yet!" Then the ASBOs was given and then who watches out for the ASBOs? Who watches out who breaches the ASBOs? The police are busy, the other agencies of the council are busy so then it's left down to the residents again. But what happens then, people stand back a bit because when that ASBO is taken you can get a professional worker to do your statement and go to court but when they breach an ASBO the actual person has to go in court. People was too intimidated because you don't know what's going to go through your door, whatever plus [at the beginning of this year] I had a warning from the youths. They broke into my house. I got told it was a warning.'

The residents and victims interviewed made repeated reference to problems of intimidation and the unwillingness of a number of victims and witnesses to come forward and give evidence. Many said that they feared reprisals, not only to themselves but also to their children. Apart from intimidation, residents made frequent reference to what they saw as the non-enforcement of breaches and the general lack of monitoring of ASBOs. In one case in which a group of residents had been persuaded to spend 18 months gathering the evidence to secure an ASBO, they were aggrieved when they saw the offender back in the area after a relatively short period. As one resident reported, in one case where a young person had been served with an ASBO and breached it:

> 'He came out of court that day and he got a £10 fine and he thought, "Right I will go on to the next stage," which he did which was theft and they gave him four months and he was out in two and he is still parading around and he is still causing ASB [anti-social behaviour]. All I get told is that if the police see him they can arrest him but I mean if a resident or local community sees him they've got to go to court but people won't do that because they are intimidated.'

In general, some residents resented being asked to be the 'eyes and ears' of the community and to take on the responsibility to gather evidence when there was such a low level of police visibility in the area. It was claimed by a number of residents' groups that when they tried to contact the local police at night there was often no reply. The residents in one borough that had a problem of street prostitution were particularly critical of the local police and to a lesser extent the local authority (Sagar, 2007). They complained that the police were slow to respond to their complaints and they were given the impression that street prostitution is not a police priority. Thus, in order to get a police response, either the residents tended to exaggerate the problem and tell the police that drug dealing was going on or they rang 999. The perceived lack of police response was seen to be damaging to police–public relations and to undermine the attempts to reduce crime and anti-social behaviour. One person who ran the local residents' group commented on the lack of an effective police response as follows:

> 'I think it also degrades the partnership. Because you think after writing X amount of e-mails that we are further down the line and why bother? So people withdraw from police partnership and say, "What's the point?'. And that builds an apathy which is very worrying.'

A lack of public engagement, of course, can make the process of gathering evidence for ASBOs or for other reasons increasingly difficult. If ASBOs are to be a cost-effective measure, community co-operation is of considerable importance. It was not only the police, however, who came in for criticism of residents. Nearly all the residents' groups expressed varying degrees of frustration in relation to the response offered by key agencies. Thus, in one focus group discussion, it was stated that:

> 'Our caretaker says he can't approach people about it [anti-social behaviour] 'cos it's not his responsibility. So you get in touch with the police and they say, "It's not our responsibility". The council have done nothing to involve us or the police. Who can we turn to?'

The general lack of support and patchy response by key agencies caused residents considerable anxiety and a number of residents said that they were ill informed and had little involvement in decision-making processes. Many felt that their opinions and experiences were largely being ignored.

Issues of displacement

Communities were also critical of what they saw as 'inconsistencies across boroughs'. Residents of one borough bordering the London Borough of Camden, which has issued the highest number of ASBOs in London, were concerned about displacement. As one female respondent, who was chair of the Sector Working Group, put it:

> 'If you have one borough coming down very strongly and your neighbourhood borough not, then you are obviously going to get a displacement of offenders. They are just going to walk away from King's Cross, which is Camden, and walk over the border into Westminster so that is a significant problem. That is why you must have consistency of ASBO approach (a) across boroughs and councils and (b) across the magistrates.'

ASBOs have also been used extensively by the British Transport Police and London Underground to prevent anti-social behaviour in and around the underground and national rail stations. Interviews with London Underground and British Transport Police employees in the course of this research indicate that while ASBOs have successfully cleared some stations of ticket touts, and both customers and staff have noticed the difference, there is still concern that the activities of some of those given ASBOs has been displaced. One London Underground employee stated:

> 'I think the ASBO was effective with these ticket touts because they are mainly drug or alcohol abusers and they need rehabilitation and possibly imprisonment or a prison hospital. They'll probably do it elsewhere, but as far as the station goes, they've gone.'

London Underground staff also reported that ASBOs had been effective in reducing the problems associated with ticket touts in a number of underground stations. One significant impact of the reduction of ticket touts, besides the decreased in levels of intimidation experienced by some members of the public, is that the reduction had served to restore confidence among station staff. One of the members of staff working in the station, however, felt that because most of the touts were addicted to drugs they would probably turn their attention to other types of activity to generate money in other locations where they were not known. He stated that:

> 'They just move to somewhere and something else. The ASBO just stops the touting, but I get the feeling that they just do something else.'

A similar situation was reported by a victim working on a large council estate. She suggested that while an ASBO may stop a particular young person from behaving badly, it does not itself address the causes of the behaviour and therefore is unlikely to provide a long-term solution. In her words:

> 'Oh the problem hasn't gone ... no, definitely not and actually there are still a couple of Peter's crowd about that basically do give me grief and there's one particular girl who is still very verbally abusive to me.... I would say it is worse than Peter's crowd. They were bored, whereas these kids now are actually malicious.'

On another housing estate, a complainant reported that an ASBO served on noisy neighbours who had been 'blighting' the estate had decreased the anti-social behaviour by removing that person from the area. She reported, however, that this had not instilled a permanent change in attitude in the offender, but rather had offered temporary relief through her absence from the neighbourhood. She said of the ASBO:

> 'Sometimes it is working and sometimes it isn't. But it is because they are not here ... when we see them, they make up for it, like.'

It was also felt by some residents that they had inherited certain individuals who had been given ASBOs in other locations and had subsequently decided to 'hang around' on neighbouring estates. As one resident put it:

> 'They [young people with ASBOs] don't hang around there anymore. They hang around here because they don't have an ASBO here. It has displaced the problem. They are hanging around smoking spliffs.'

Concern for the vulnerable and marginalised

While the use of ASBOs in some anti-social behaviour 'hotspots' was reported to have had a positive effect on the quality of life of local residents (at least in the short term), there were considerable reservations about the effects on the individuals, particularly those with problems of homelessness, alcohol and drug dependency. Overall, many respondents were concerned with the exclusionary and marginalising effects of ASBOs, in some cases feeling compassion for those about whom they had complained. In the case study below, which outlines the use of ASBOs and other measures to address street prostitution, it is interesting to note that while the priority for the residents was reducing the level of prostitution, they justified the use of ASBOs in terms of the potential support that the women concerned would receive when issued with an ASBO. Thus it was suggested that:

> 'These girls will get much more help if they are in that system of ASBOs. They can get drug rehab and they can get social security caring.'

It was also suggested that even if the sex workers breached the ASBO and went to prison, it could be beneficial, because they could receive help with their drug addiction in prison. Similar rationales were presented during the course of the focus groups, with residents in some cases echoing the views of certain practitioners to the effect that ASBOs could constitute a positive intervention in the lives of people like drug addicts, because it could set in motion a change of behaviour, particularly if the appropriate support services were activated. One victim, when asked by a member of the Youth Offending Team (YOT) what she would like to see happen to a young offender who had intimidated her and stolen her mobile phone, said:

> 'What about some sort of educational programme or apprenticeship where at least they are doing something instead of just coming once a week to report to you.'

The victim in this case added that the YOT officer had promised to keep her in touch with the progress of this particular young person. However, she reported no further communication from the YOT. On another council estate, residents complained of what they saw as the local councils making promises in relation to intervention that have not materialised. In particular, they claimed that they saw little evidence of money and resources being provided for the disadvantaged young people living in and around the estate. There were complaints that although local authorities made claims about the work that they were doing in the neighbourhood to reduce anti-social behaviour, there was little sign of targeted intervention. As one resident stated:

> 'I think it's ridiculous and I don't know where they are putting the money to help these ASB kids because I tell you something they are not putting it on this estate or neighbouring estates.'

There was a widespread consensus that the pursuit of an ASBO should be accompanied by the mobilisation of additional support measures. While residents want relief from noise, harassment and nuisance, they want to see ASBOs linked to rehabilitative measures, particularly to address problematic drug and alcohol use.

Competing priorities

The issue of local versus national priorities was raised by the focus groups. It was felt that the priorities for the police and local authorities were set by government and that local communities did not have much opportunity to determine priorities for their area. The police, in particular, were seen to be at fault in this respect. As one, rather irate, resident put it:

> 'It is certainly the fault of the police and as long as you have these talked-down priorities from the Home Office, not equating with the local and community needs, you do have an open warfare on the streets.'

The residents felt that issuing one ASBO against a perpetrator was going to make little difference to the problems in the area. They were critical of the police, and the police in turn tended to blame the council. In an interview with the anti-social coordinator for the borough, he confirmed the anxieties of the residents and joined them in criticising the police for not gathering the necessary evidence for ASBOs.

The interviews with victims as well as the focus groups brought out some ongoing differences between the priorities and interests of local residents, practitioners and central government. Although reference was often made to focusing on local priorities, a number of victims and residents felt that both central government and certain agencies were too directive and too ready to impose their conceptions of ASB on local neighbourhoods. While official reports claim, for example, that the solution to the problem of definition of ASB is to be solved by developing local priorities, residents were more than aware that the *categories* that structure the ASB agenda are constructed by central government. At the same time, agency representatives complained that they were constrained by central government to achieve certain targets within a framework laid out by central government. Thus in relation to ASB, and by implication the pursuit of ASBOs, there appears to be an ongoing tension between local and national concerns.

Street prostitution: a case study

The situation: In an area that had been identified as a 'red-light' district for many years, the local residents had formed an action group in order to try to reduce the level of street prostitution. Located close to a main line station and a busy shopping and tourist area, this locality had a large number of hotels and visitors. Local residents claimed that in recent years the nature of street prostitution had changed in a number of significant ways in that it was becoming more aggressive, with frequent street fights, that the vast majority of the sex workers were addicted to drugs, and that the period of operation now carried on through the night into the early morning, keeping residents awake. At the same time, the area was becoming increasingly gentrified, with an increasing number of owner-occupiers living in increasingly expensive properties.

The intervention: Over the past decade, the residents' group had put consistent pressure on the police and the local authority to 'clean up the streets'. The police had responded by developing a range of interventions, but they had not managed to reduce the level of street prostitution and related issues of noise and litter. The residents claimed that the fines given to those prostitutes arrested by the police were ineffective and possibly counterproductive and did not act as an effective deterrent. Residents had tried to address the issue by installing gates and CCTV. The residents themselves had contributed to the cost of these developments. They complain that the police were slow to respond to their complaints, and they had got the impression that street prostitution was not a police priority. Thus, in order to get a police response, the residents either exaggerated the problem and told the police that drug dealing was going on, or they rang 999.

The impact: The perceived ineffectiveness of the various measures adopted by the residents and the police resulted in growing support in the locality for the use of ASBOs, which the residents felt would give them some immediate relief from the noise and disturbance associated with street prostitution and possibly deter a number of sex workers. The use of ASBOs was justified by both the residents and the police, who claimed that the issuing of an ASBO or a resulting prison sentence might instigate some form of treatment or support for the sex workers.

An assessment: However, after more than two years of pursuing ASBOs for sex workers only one had been issued. Another order that was processed was later dismissed on a technicality by the court. The ASBO that was issued was breached a number of times, but it seems that the person concerned had moved from the area; the researchers could not locate her and the relevant agencies appeared to know little about her whereabouts or her wellbeing. The residents felt that the one ASBO that had been issued had made little or no difference and felt that only a series of ASBOs would be effective in significantly reducing the level of street prostitution.

Recently, the council had directed its attention at kerb crawlers and had threatened to serve Acceptable Behaviour Contracts on them and to take away their driving licences. The residents welcomed this initiative, which included a 'naming and shaming' component. Although they were generally frustrated by the limited commitment by the police, they were well organised and well resourced and would no doubt continue to campaign on all fronts.

Conclusion

5

This has been an exploratory study based on a selective sample of offenders, agencies, victims and residents. It became evident in the course of the research that these different groups tended to employ different criteria of 'success' in relation to the use of Anti-Social Behaviour Orders (ASBOs). Assessments of success tended to be made on a number of dimensions:

- bringing relief to certain neighbourhoods and groups;
- reducing the level and impact of anti-social behaviour;
- changing attitudes and motivation of offenders;
- level of breaches and their enforcement;
- reduction of different forms of anti-social behaviour in the area.

In relation to these different options, it was the view among various respondents that ASBOs had in some cases been effective in bringing at least temporary relief to certain neighbourhoods and groups. Where ASBOs had been served in series on various 'ringleaders', they were seen to be effective in reducing certain forms of anti-social behaviour or group disorder, although it often took a relatively long period of time and considerable resources to achieve this result. It was also felt that in some cases alternative and more appropriate sanctions could have been used to resolve issues in a less punitive way.

The impact on offenders was more positive than may have been expected, with 43% indicating some improvement in their offending behaviour and a similar percentage acknowledging a positive change of attitude after receiving an ASBO – sometimes in quite fundamental ways. However, this does not necessarily indicate a direct causal link between the intervention and the outcomes. In some cases, there were changes in specific forms of behaviour without any change in attitudes towards engaging in crime or anti-social behaviour in general. Some changes appeared to be a function of a normal maturation process, with young people 'growing out of crime' at a certain point in their lives. Some offenders improved as a result of other support measures mobilised alongside the ASBO, while for others changing relations with peers and family were a significant factor. It was reported, however, that the mental state and social circumstances of those given ASBOs sometimes worsened, while many experienced difficulties finding employment.

Over half (59%) of those given ASBOs admitted that they had breached the conditions, with one in six saying that they had breached on more than three occasions. We developed a typology of 'success' for each offender and found that approximately one third reported an improvement in behaviour and offending, 15% reported a decrease in the level of their substance abuse and 14% said that they had experienced some improvement in their mental state. Only 3% of offenders reported any improvement of their social circumstances following the imposition of the ASBO. Of some concern was the finding that some 28% reported some deterioration in their mental state after receiving an ASBO.

It was apparent from the review of the cases included in the research that a critical factor in determining the impact of ASBOs was the provision of support and welfare services to perpetrators. It was found that many of those interviewed suffered from a range of psychological, social and economic problems and there was a widespread consensus that ASBOs were more likely to be effective when linked to the appropriate support measures. However, there was a suspicion among some respondents that rather than ASBOs being a trigger for setting in motion a range of support measures, either before or after the ASBO was served, they could too easily be used as a way of agencies 'washing their hands' of troublesome and time-consuming individuals and in some cases of deliberately displacing problem groups into other areas.

Alongside the issue of breaches, concerns were expressed by different agency representatives and residents' groups in relation to the conditions contained in ASBOs. It was widely felt that the conditions were often inappropriate and unenforceable and that guidelines need to be developed to overcome this problem. In cases where the conditions were seen as extreme, either by the agencies, the public or the media, the credibility of ASBOs was called into question. There were concerns expressed by both practitioners and residents in relation to the monitoring of cases, which was seen to be patchy in most boroughs and virtually non-existent in others.

A further issue that requires urgent attention is the displacement effects – both geographic and functional – of ASBOs. Since the number of ASBOs issued is increasing apace and since the majority of orders include an element of geographic displacement – in some cases beyond borough boundaries – there is a need to assess the impact of ASBOs on surrounding areas. This purposive displacement makes the task of assessing the impact of ASBOs on the general level of ASB difficult to assess. While the consistent use of ASBOs might be linked to a reduction of anti-social behaviour in one borough, it might increase anti-social behaviour in surrounding boroughs. Thus evaluations of the impact of ASBOs on the general level of ASB will require a methodology that moves beyond empiricism and involves a demonstration of causal connections.

In general, it should be noted in future research that aims to address the question of whether or not ASBOs work that there are three important dimensions to this question that need to be addressed. The first is who is selected for an ASBO or an ASBO on Conviction (CRASBO)? The criteria of selection are critical to the potential effectiveness of these orders. Clearly, if stand-alone ASBOs or CRASBOs are used for inappropriate groups of offenders, or at an inappropriate point in their offending histories, their likelihood of success will be limited. We have tried to indicate in this study which groups of offenders are likely to respond both positively and negatively to ASBOs. Second, in relation to 'what works', the ways in which the orders are framed and implemented will have a major impact on their success or otherwise. Including conditions that are inappropriate or excessive can all too easily undermine the potential effectiveness and credibility of these orders. Third, the issue of 'what works' cannot be answered satisfactorily until more robust forms of monitoring and assessment are put in place. At the moment, the level of monitoring and evaluation appears to be extremely low and therefore the effectiveness of ASBOs in most areas remains uncertain. Any future research that makes the claim that ASBOs 'work' without thoroughly examining these three dimensions, and how they effect outcomes, should be treated with extreme caution.

The increased use of CRASBOs, while avoiding the costly and time-consuming processes associated with pursuing a case conference approach, is likely to have significant implications for the selection of offenders served with ASBOs as well as the enforcement and monitoring of orders. It is evident that their use has also created tensions and uncertainties in partnership working, with certain agencies complaining that they are not always being informed that a CRASBO is being sought.

It is also the case that as the use of ASBOs increases, more attention will need to be paid to the use of other sanctions and interventions that have been developed to deal with anti-social behaviour either by themselves or in combination with ASBOs. The considerable publicity surrounding ASBOs and the relative ease with which CRASBOs can be administered may result in ASBOs increasingly becoming the sanction of first resort rather than last resort, while related measures remain underused.

In relation to the growing use of ASBOs and their mixed and uncertain impact, the research indicates that in a significant percentage of cases offending stopped or decreased at the point that offenders were informed that an ASBO had been sought. In some cases, the offender's attitude and behaviour had changed dramatically before they appeared in court and the ASBO was issued. This finding suggests that it might be prudent to use warnings more strategically and to monitor closely the response of offenders before instigating court proceedings. In general, the development of a more incremental and structured approach to dealing with anti-social behaviour would seem worthy of further consideration.

There can be little doubt that the considerable media coverage given to ASBOs, both positive and negative, has drawn attention to their use. The high profile of ASBOs has almost certainly influenced levels of social tolerance and sensitised the public to a range of issues while serving as a general deterrent. The publicity surrounding anti-social behaviour campaigns has also increased the public expectation that these issues can be addressed effectively. We noted in our survey of victims and residents' groups that even where noticeable improvements had taken place, there remained considerable dissatisfaction and criticism of the authorities.

There is already some recognition that the design and implementation of ASBOs is in need of some revision (Home Office, 2006). There are plans to develop clearer guidelines for magistrates and Crown Courts to deal with ASBOs more quickly and efficiently. At the same time, the possibility of widening the range of authorities that are empowered to issue ASBOs is now under consideration. There is also a commitment to reviewing the duration of ASBOs. However, as this report suggests, there are further issues that need to be addressed if the appropriateness, utility and credibility of ASBOs is to be improved.

References

Ashworth, H. (2004) 'Social Control and "Anti-social behaviour": The Subversion of Human Rights', *Law Quarterly Review*, vol 120, pp 263-91, April.

Burney, E. (2002) 'Talking tough: acting coy: what happened to the Anti-Social Behaviour Order?', *The Howard Journal*, vol 4, no 5, pp 469-84.

Campbell, S. (2002a) *A Review of Anti-Social Behaviour Orders*, Home Office Research Study 236, London: Home Office.

Campbell, S. (2002b) *Implementing Anti-Social Behaviour Orders: Messages for Practitioners*, Home Office Findings 160, London: Home Office.

Floud, S. (2005) 'Asbolands? A study of Anti-Social Behaviour Orders in the London boroughs', Unpublished MSc Dissertation, London School of Economics and Political Science.

GLA (Greater London Authority) (2005) *The London Anti-Social Behaviour Strategy 2005-08*, London: GLA.

Home Affairs Committee (2005) *Anti-Social Behaviour. Fifth Report of Session 2004-2005*, London: The Stationery Office.

Home Office (2003) *Respect and Responsibility – Taking a Stand Against Anti-Social Behaviour*, London: The Stationery Office.

Home Office (2004) *Defining and Measuring Anti-Social Behaviour*, London: The Stationery Office.

Home Office (2005) *Anti-Social Behaviour: The Government Reply to the Fifth Report from the Home Affairs Committee Session 2004-05*, Cm 6588, London: The Stationery Office.

Home Office (2006) *Respect Action Plan*, London: The Stationery Office.

Isal, S. (2006) *Equal Respect – ASBO and Race Equality*, London: The Runnymede Trust.

Koffman, L. (2006) 'The use of Anti-Social Behaviour Orders: an empirical study of a New Deal for Communities area', *Criminal Law Review*, July, pp 593-613.

London Assembly (2005) *Street Prostitution in London*, London: GLA.

Lord Justice Thomas (2005) *Anti-Social Behaviour Orders: A Guide on ASBOs for Judges Sitting in the Magistrates, Crown and County Courts*, London: The Stationery Office.

National Audit Office (2006) *The Home Office: Tackling Anti-Social Behaviour*, London: The Stationery Office.

Sagar, T. (2007) 'Tackling on-street sex work: Anti-Social Behaviour Orders, sex workers and inclusive inter-agency initiatives', *Criminology and Criminal Justice*, vol 7, pp 153-68.

Scottish Executive (2005) *Use of Anti-Social Behaviour Orders in Scotland*, Edinburgh: DTZ Pieda Consulting and Heriot Watt University.

Solanki, A.-R., Bateman, T., Boswell, G. and Hill, E. (2006) *Anti-Social Behaviour Orders*, London: Youth Justice Board.

Squires, P. and Stephen, D. (2005) 'Rethinking ASBOs', *Critical Social Policy*, vol 25, no 4, pp 517-28.

Young, T., Hallsworth, S., Jackson, A. and Lindsey, J. (2006) *Crime Displacement in King's Cross: Report for Camden Community Safety Partnership*, London: Centre for Social and Evaluation Research, London Metropolitan University.